ENDING CHECKBOX DIVERSITY

Rewriting the Story of Performative Allyship in Corporate America

ENDING CHECKBOX DIVERSITY

DANNIE LYNN FOUNTAIN

BK

Berrett–Koehler Publishers, Inc

Berrett-Koehler Publishers, Inc.
1333 Broadway, Suite 1000
Oakland, CA 94612-1921
Tel: (510) 817-2277
Fax: (510) 817-2278
www.bkconnection.com

ORDERING INFORMATION

Quantity sales. Special discounts are available on quantity purchases by corporations, associations, and others. For details, contact the "Special Sales Department" at the Berrett-Koehler address above.

Individual sales. Berrett-Koehler publications are available through most bookstores. They can also be ordered directly from Berrett-Koehler:

Tel: (800) 929-2929; Fax: (802) 864-7626; www.bkconnection.com.

Orders for college textbook / course adoption use. Please contact Berrett-Koehler: Tel: (800) 929-2929; Fax: (802) 864-7626.

Distributed to the US trade and internationally by Penguin Random House Publisher Services.

Berrett-Koehler and the BK logo are registered trademarks of Berrett-Koehler Publishers, Inc.

Printed in Canada

Berrett-Koehler books are printed on long-lasting acid-free paper. When it is available, we choose paper that has been manufactured by environmentally responsible processes. These may include using trees grown in sustainable forests, incorporating recycled paper, minimizing chlorine in bleaching, or recycling the energy produced at the paper mill.

Library of Congress Cataloging-in-Publication Data

Names: Fountain, Dannie Lynn, author.
Title: Ending checkbox diversity : rewriting the story of performative
   allyship in corporate America / Dannie Lynn Fountain.
Description: First edition. | Oakland, CA : Berrett-Koehler Publishers,
   [2023] | Includes bibliographical references and index.
Identifiers: LCCN 2022014862 (print) | LCCN 2022014863 (ebook) |
   ISBN 9781523001354 (paperback) | ISBN 9781523001361 (pdf) |
   ISBN 9781523001378 (epub) | ISBN 9781523001392
Subjects: LCSH: Diversity in the workplace—United States. |
   Multiculturalism—United States. | Discrimination in employment—
   United States.
Classification: LCC HF5549.5.M5 F687 2023 (print) | LCC HF5549.5.M5
   (ebook) | DDC 331.13/30973—dc23/eng/20220716
LC record available at https://lccn.loc.gov/2022014862
LC ebook record available at https://lccn.loc.gov/2022014863

First Edition

27 26 25 24 23 22   10 9 8 7 6 5 4 3 2 1

Book producer: Susan Geraghty
Cover designer: Sophie Greenbaum
Interior design: Lewelin Polanco
Author photo: Catherine Lavy, Lavybug Photography
Art featured in author photo: Alannah Tiller, aLILscribble

To everyone who has ever had
to fight for basic respect at work.

You deserve a far better world.

Contents

Before You Read

(A Note from the Author)

While these pages tell the tale of modern-day Corporate America's experiences and failures with DEI, they also hold the impact, trauma, and outcomes of my own experiences as an "other" navigating this country's white-collar, buttoned up, still-too-stodgy offices. I've removed some personal details, not to protect those within the stories, but rather so you might more easily find your own experiences mirrored or magnified in mine.

Every personal story and public news piece discussed in this book is written from my perspective, the way I remember it happening, through my lens as a human defined by the many labels assigned to me by society.* Your labels might be different. You might shoulder more; you might be burdened by less. You might remember these stories differently depending on your perception of the situation. Your reactions

---

* You might find yourself wondering what exactly my labels are. Although many of our labels change over time, based on our own self-concept and those created by our society, here is a brief list of some of my labels at the time of writing: queer, multiethnic, neurodivergent, heavily tattooed, married, plus-size, first-generation, cisgender, woman. I was raised in a lower-class household and currently am a debt-free member of the upper class.

to these stories and suggestions for what to do next might be different than mine. In fact, reading this book might make you feel angry, frustrated, discouraged, or a myriad of other heavy negative emotions.

I encourage you to sit with how you feel before you react. Consider whether your reaction is to the words I've put on these pages or to thoughts, feelings, and experiences within your own existence that have been magnified by the book you hold in your hands. Know that the weight of your own experiences is not a weight you've created but one that Corporate America has set on your shoulders. And if you feel light, not bogged down by the heaviness of the tales herein, consider why that might be.

And above all else, I encourage you more than anything to take action not just when this book ends but along the way. Make notes in the margins, snap photos and text to friends, read passages aloud to your partner as you consider your own experiences in Corporate America. Once you've done that, consider how these words might leave the page, how they can spark deeper conversations in your organization. Let the words move you toward **change**.

Dannie Lynn Fountain

Laying the
Groundwork

Trigger warnings for this book: sexual harassment, racism, various discussions of discrimination and workplace acts of aggression.

Quick definition: Throughout this book, we will use the terms *underrepresented identities, marginalized individuals,* and *minorities* somewhat interchangeably. These three terms have varying definitions, but all are used within this text to reference any individual who holds an identity, belief, or experience that is contrary to or separate from the majority norms of the "white experience" in Corporate America. An individual may be a member of one of these groups (i.e., marginalized) but not another (i.e., underrepresented) and still experience harm in Corporate America.

What do you do when your company claims to care about diversity, equity, and inclusion (DEI), but is also incredibly successful at discriminating against or ignoring your identities?

The answer for many underrepresented folks is to feel defeated, wonder whether they made the right career choice, second-guess every accomplishment that got them to where they are, and generally feel overwhelmed and exhausted. The answer for me? A little bit of that defeated feeling, but a much more pronounced urge to rage against the system. It may be the Enneagram 8 in me (the Challenger), or more likely it's that underlying feeling held by every person who has an underrepresented identity—the powerful desire to join the ever-present battle to gain just a smidgen of ground closer to equity.

◾

I've been in Corporate America for nearly a decade now, and as an underrepresented triple minority who passes for a straight white woman, I've seen and heard a lot of things that corporations would prefer I hadn't. This experience as a "wolf in sheep's clothing" reaffirms our understanding that all too often, DEI initiatives are motivated by profit, not respect for humanity.

◾

This book is the story of Corporate America's DEI duality. As someone who started their career in marketing and now works in HR, I have seen this duality firsthand. The creation of marketing campaigns on the basis of the sales they might garner instead of on the basis of celebrating the represented communities is all too common. Highlighting underrepresented individuals in company marketing materials and then failing to pay them equitably or offer them career advancement opportunities is the norm. The same individuals on billboards in Times Square or front and center during a Super Bowl commercial have been discriminated against, sexually harassed, and openly harmed, while corporate policy enforcers fail to respond appropriately because the incident didn't "rise to the level" of what the policy protects.

◾

From the outside looking in, DEI initiatives are on-trend; they make for great PR fodder and really separate the inclusive companies from the outright discriminatory ones. That's not actually the truth, though. DEI is rarely a true priority, rarely receives equitable capital investment, and rarely has consistent and unilateral leadership buy-in. As a result, DEI initiatives are underfunded, underreported, and generally have underwhelming performance as a result, all while companies continue to discriminate against and actively harm their underrepresented employees.

It's possible that you picked up this book because you feel the pain of this duality as much as I do. You might also be wrestling with the same questions I am: Is Ramsey Solutions (Dave Ramsey's financial empire) somehow a better company than the tech industry giants because at least Ramsey Solutions is transparent about what (or who) its priorities actually are? Ramsey Solutions is consistently discriminatory toward underrepresented identities (see: the lawsuits that just keep coming), whereas the tech industry's only consistency is in its murkiness of discrimination and active harm while also investing in DEI.

Or maybe you picked up this book because you're a leader who is not sure what to do. You know that current efforts are failing, but you don't have the background or context to begin to figure out what happens next.

Regardless of why you picked up this book, I'm glad you're here. This nuanced discussion of DEI at the highest echelons of Corporate America will empower you to take your career into your own hands and maybe even spark ~~some change~~ an uprising.

However, this isn't just a story of how messed up corporate DEI currently is; it's also a hard look at just the beginning of what it takes to get DEI right.

▣

As we dig into part I, we'll have a frank conversation about the current context of diversity initiatives in Corporate America. The identity of America is changing, the country is becoming majority-minority, and underrepresented groups now hold immense economic power, yet DEI initiatives at major companies are deprioritized or largely relegated to volunteer committees led by underrepresented individuals themselves.

▣

We'll explore how the current structure of corporate DEI lends itself to the continued oppression of and discrimination against underrepresented identities. We'll examine the narrow objectives and key results (OKR) metrics that allow for shallow or no improvement year after year. We'll also take a look at how employee turnover and the shifting of diversity responsibility to employee resource groups allows companies to disclaim responsibility for making meaningful progress.

▣

In part II, we'll talk about the "why now"—why this conversation is shifting today and why the current DEI efforts are no longer good enough. We'll evaluate the events of 2020 that have incited an awakening that can no longer be ignored and have elevated the expectations for Corporate America. We'll also talk about the impact of Xennials and Gen Zers on the workforce as America's most diverse and mixed-race generation(s) ever. Finally, we'll work through some of the most notable (and publicized) examples of poor DEI initiatives and corporate inclusion failings with a breakdown of how and why they were so ineffective (and what they might have done differently).

In part III, we'll try to fix the mess laid out in the first two parts of the book. We'll inevitably fail, because no one book can solve the complex issues of Corporate America, but we'll take steps forward. We'll build a roadmap for what to do instead, what DEI actually looks like, and how to avoid the performative allyship trope.

By the time you finish this book, you will, I hope, have a better understanding of exactly how Corporate America is failing underrepresented identities and a plan for what to do next. You'll be armed with clear examples and metrics for evaluating DEI in your own career and workplace, enabling you to align with and work for companies that are actually doing the work. You'll also have the tools you need to chase after meaningful DEI in your own organization.

Ready to actually give a shit about humanity? Let's do this.

ENDING CHECKBOX DIVERSITY

Introduction

Why Now?

Diversity, equity, and inclusion (DEI) is nothing new in the corporate space. Employee resource groups (ERGs) were one of the first avenues where underrepresented employees could access representation and opportunities for community among underrepresented identities. The first ERG was founded in the 1960s when Black workers at Xerox came together to discuss race-based tension in the workplace and what options they had to address it.

▣

What is new, however, is the incredibly powerful yet disgusting dichotomy between DEI initiatives that are publicly presented as authentic moves toward better representation, and the internal politics and unspoken rules that lend themselves to ongoing discrimination and exclusion. Companies today are able to do both: publicly represent themselves as powerful DEI allies while also privately discriminating against their underrepresented employee base in painful and deeply harmful ways.

▣

This book is the story of Corporate America's DEI duality. DEI is just one part of corporate social responsibility and is not viewed as inherently profitable the way that renewable resources and recycling are. Only initiatives that demonstrate financial gains receive strong investments. Instead of prioritizing respect for one another and a safe working environment (both of which are outcomes of DEI work), Corporate America is underfunding and underreporting DEI and employee representation. Unpacking the motivation behind this helps understand why checkbox diversity became a norm in the first place.

◼

There is no better time than now, no better moment than this one, to begin to truly understand the tremendous amount of damage that Corporate America has done to the underrepresented population in this country. At the same time, while DEI initiatives have the public ear for a moment, it's critical to take this opportunity to implement changes that will heal some of the harm and create a better future for our rising new generation of workforce contributors.

◼

This book is full of hard conversations and painful stories, but it's also full of hope, light, and meaningful opportunities for corporate leaders to take responsibility and enact change. Although the tone of this book often comes across as "Let's tear down Corporate America;" it's actually a "Corporate America, this is your last opportunity to change" kind of book.

How Did We Get Here?

Underrepresented individuals of their respective eras have been fighting for inclusion for centuries—from ancient quests to combat injustice to the more recent examples of the last one hundred years. Prior to the Declaration of Independence in 1776 and for many years after, US common law (inherited from the British) was often hostile toward labor rights. Despite these fights, it has been a slow crawl to enshrine formal protections for a myriad of underrepresented identities in official US labor laws.

The first modern attempt at equal employment in a formal way was Executive Order 9981, signed in 1948 by President Truman, desegregating the military. Within five years of the order's being signed, 95 percent of Black army soldiers in the US were serving in integrated units, a unique and isolated success story for checkbox diversity. However, not everyone would celebrate the success of this integration, and Black soldiers were far from treated equitably.

In the 1960s, civil rights legislation prohibited discrimination on the basis of race, color, religion, sex, national origin, and, later, age. Title VII specifically prohibits "discrimination in hiring, promotion, discharge, pay, fringe benefits, job training, classification, referral, and other aspects of employment, on the basis of race, color, religion, sex or national origin." (Though to be clear—Title VII does not apply to all companies and therefore does not protect all underrepresented groups from prohibited discrimination.) The Equal Pay Act of 1963 requires companies to pay women the same amount they would pay men for doing the same job (although many would correctly argue that we are still far from achieving this).

In 1978, the Pregnancy Discrimination Act was signed, prohibiting discrimination against hiring or continued employment based on pregnancy.

In 1987, a government study of economic and demographic trends was commissioned; the resulting report highlighted five key demographic factors central to the US labor market. These five factors became the basis for modern-day diversity initiatives in the workplace.[1] These factors indicated important changes impacting the way that companies conduct workforce planning, including that more women and underrepresented individuals will enter the workforce and immigrants will likely represent the largest share of the increase in workforce (as measured since World War I).

◳

The Americans with Disabilities Act (ADA) became law in 1990, prohibiting discrimination against individuals with disabilities in a myriad of areas, including the workplace.

◳

The Family and Medical Leave Act was passed in 1993, protecting eligible families who need to take time off work for medical conditions or to take care of a newborn child.

◳

These movements paved the way for the changes we've seen in the twenty-first century:

- ► The Lilly Ledbetter Fair Pay Act of 2009 reaffirmed and amended much of Title VII and provided discriminated individuals more protections in filing a claim.
- ► The Me Too Act was signed in 2017, offering expanded protections against sexual harassment and discrimination in the workplace.
- ► In June 2020, the Supreme Court ruled that individuals could no longer be fired for being gay or transgender (providing additional protections to some but not all members of the LGBTQIA+ community).

These and dozens of other federal laws (roughly 180 in total), Supreme Court cases, and state legislative actions have expanded protections in

Corporate America for underrepresented identities of every shape and size throughout the past hundred years. (It is important to note that white women have been the primary beneficiaries of most affirmative action improvements; in the two decades after the launch of affirmative action, white women have experienced better pay and more senior career advancement than other women.)[2] Despite this protection, we still see devastating and often unilateral discrimination and anti-inclusion actions in the workplace.

What's Actually Happening in the Workplace

There have been more than 1.8 million complaints filed with the Equal Employment Opportunity Commission since 1997.[3] This agency, established in 1964, administers and enforces laws related to workplace discrimination. This category of complaint also has the lowest rate of success—only 15 percent of complainants ever receive any form of relief, and fewer than 1 percent of the complaints had a discrimination finding.[4] Nearly half of those claims (710,500) were filed in one category: color and race. Still today, the total number of color and race discrimination charges is higher than any other category of complaints. Despite dozens of laws enacted since 1997 to offer greater workplace protections, there has been no major decrease in complaints during that time.

◻

This creates a devastating experience for underrepresented workers in Corporate America. Three in five US employees (regardless of their identity) have witnessed or experienced discrimination based on a protected category, as of a study completed in 2019.[5] The current gender wage gap still has a delta of nearly 20 percent, with Latinx women making just $0.54 to a white man's dollar.[6] (This gap costs women millions in salary and investment gains over a forty-year career, and at the current pace, won't be closed before 2059.) One in four Black workers reports discrimination at work (and nearly all fear reporting, in case of retribution). Millennial Black and Latinx employees experience discrimination at the highest rates (31 percent), nearly double that of the same-age white workers.

◻

All of this sounds scary, but why aren't employees speaking up? Well, employee engagement in a workplace is directly linked to how an employee believes their employer would respond to discrimination concerns—and that confidence is stunningly low.[7] Confidence is further harmed by the outcomes of speaking up—the justified fear of retaliation, loss of career prospects internally (and if publicized, externally), and the corresponding loss to income and other elements of financial security. This lack of confidence leads to attrition, the cost of which to both the employee *and* employer is startling. The employee has to start over, searching for a new job under less than ideal conditions, while also trying to heal their own trauma and mental health related to the discrimination. Employers on the whole rarely change their ways and end up spending more than $64 billion annually to replace employees who departed due to discrimination.[8] Which brings us to . . .

Why Change Now?

The real question is "Why not?!" but not every company has come to that conclusion yet. Much of today's research that is used as a motivator to encourage companies to do the right thing is centered on topics of financial and innovation impacts. These motivators include data points such as the following:

▦

Accenture conducted a study in 2019 which found that corporate cultures of equality are powerful multipliers of innovation and growth. Specifically, "innovation mindset" (the willingness and ability to innovate) is six times higher in equal cultures versus unequal ones. In fact, Accenture calculated that the global GDP would increase by $8 trillion if the innovation mindset rose by 10 percent in every country.

॰

Diversity has specific, tangible, and near-term business impacts too— companies report 53 percent greater performance when they have female board directors[9] and 35 percent greater financial returns with racial and ethnic diversity.[10]

॰

Beyond business impact is the influence that diversity has on opportunities to shatter industry norms. The standpoint theory suggests that underrepresented individuals bring fresh or different perspectives to companies, primarily due to the ways that their worldview differs from that of the dominant identity group.[11] The conversations sparked from these differing viewpoints are often what lead to new products or consumer solutions that change the market entirely. Without diversity of thought in the C-suite, many a product launch never would have happened.

॰

But finances and innovation aren't the only reasons to prioritize DEI. In fact, they really shouldn't be the central reasons at all. Using business cases, financial outcomes, and proclamations of innovations as the reasons to focus on DEI centers the company's outcomes—predicating the respectful and equitable treatment of all employees on the ability of that treatment to turn a profit. The reality is that every single person in the workplace, or who desires to be in the workplace, has a right to a workplace that is free of harassment, free of mistreatment, and free of barriers to advancement. *This* is the core tenet and motivator for why companies should adopt DEI practices. Giving a shit about humanity is the best kind of business practice Corporate America could ever adopt.

| PART I |

The Historical Context of Corporate DEI

ONE

Where Did DEI Come From?

In many ways, Corporate America's relationship with taking action to address DEI metrics (or trying to improve inclusion at all) began in the 1980s and '90s with sensitivity trainings. These trainings focused on a single session highlighting the differences between employees and how to "acknowledge" these differences—and typically ended with a "hug it out" moment. The knowledge was promptly put on the shelf and forgotten by the workplace majority members whom the training was meant to impact most. It's not surprising to learn that this type of training is now known to be ineffective, and even the term *sensitivity training* is no longer used.

▣

In the late 1990s and early 2000s, as more and more sex-based discrimination lawsuits were being filed and settled for massive sums of money, Corporate America as a whole began to care more about DEI. In fact, these lawsuits had a twofold impact—DEI training rose in the list of HR requirements, and so did the expectation that employees sign arbitration agreements as part of accepting their offer letters.

Unfortunately, these DEI trainings aren't doing what they're supposed to. Corporate America is naturally most concerned with checking boxes to prevent liability and litigation. As a result, these trainings are typically just a "cover our asses" move to point to in the case of a discrimination claim from an employee. "But wait, how could we have discriminated against you when we have these comprehensive inclusion trainings?!"

Today, we're using much of the same DEI initiatives and research that were first created in the 1960s, and it's not working. In fact, three of the most common diversity interventions used in Corporate America today (diversity training, grievance procedures, and standardized performance rating processes) make firms less diverse, because managers are resistant to perceived strong-arming.[1] The methodologies for furthering DEI initiatives in the workplace today break down into three specific categories.

Employee Resource Group Lobbying

The oldest form of DEI initiative in the workplace is the employee resource group (ERG). Founded at first for a sense of community but later leveraged as an opportunity to voice needs and identify disparities, today they offer a space for sharing voices, staving off isolation, and providing a collective reprieve. ERGs offer tremendous benefits to the organizations that host them—leadership development and increased retention rates, educational opportunities, recruitment, pipeline development, and so much more.

The downside of ERGs for employees is tremendous. Leading or organizing an ERG is largely volunteer work that often goes unrecognized in performance and promotion conversations. ERG budgets are often limited (and were decreased further in 2020 and beyond thanks to COVID-19 and the idea that virtual events cost less money—more on this in the next paragraph). Leadership changes over often, and continuity can be stifled with employee departures. The massive amount of emotional labor that ERG members and leaders undergo in educating the broader corporate community cannot be understated either—sometimes even joining an ERG is akin to waving a flag saying "I'm open for your identity-related Q&A."

As COVID-19 prompted a move to primarily virtual events for ERGs, many companies reduced the budget allocated to ERG programming,[2] despite many of these same groups needing community now more than ever. This reduction in budget collided head-on with misconceptions around virtual events. Pre-COVID, the prevailing belief was that you could pay the same speaker less money for a virtual event because they didn't have to travel and the work was "easier"—but they likely were putting the same amount of labor into producing the content they shared, and virtual presentations are not without their own moderation and engagement issues. As COVID hit, this belief prevailed, and speakers who could once command $15,000–$20,000 per speaking engagement were now being offered $1,000 for a virtual event, *if they were lucky*. This reduction in budget cost many ERGs the opportunity to host impactful speakers or to pay those speakers appropriately for their expertise and labor. More specifically, within the ERG space, many of these speakers held one or more marginalized identities, further compounding the impact of COVID on their livelihood.

As a whole, ERGs are often entirely undervalued for what they do for an organization. ERGs often bring tens or hundreds of thousands (if not millions) of dollars of profit to an organization[3] while operating on budgets with which most community groups couldn't even fill an event snack table. ERGs within an organization are also often not equally funded, furthering the inequity and access to opportunity. With this in mind, there are certainly ways to refresh the ways we create community for underrepresented employees at work.

Grassroots-Led Initiatives

Employee activists are becoming increasingly common as social issues come to the forefront of society. Nearly four in ten employees in Corporate America today identify as employee activists and stand willing to call out their employers publicly.[4] Furthermore, 95 percent of companies expect a rise in the number of employees using Twitter (and other platforms) to raise complaints and concerns.[5]

◼

Recent examples of employee activism include the 2018 Google Walkout (a response to executive accountability regarding sexual harassment); the 2019 Walmart Walkout (after a mass shooting at a Walmart in Texas); the 2019 Wayfair Walkout (in response to furnishing migrant holding facilities); and countless 2020–2021 protests and petitions in the face of COVID-19-related responses and working conditions.

◼

Although 2021 was characterized as the year of the labor shortage (read: actually a wage shortage), it would be more accurate to characterize it as the year of organizing. The year saw employees of all kinds, union and nonunion, bolstered by strength in numbers and the growing awareness of workplace conditions. Alongside the organizing movement was a record number of "quits" (workers who sought new jobs with better pay and working conditions), tallying more than four million throughout the year.[6] What makes 2021 even more unusual is the growing diversification of industries represented by strikes; it was one of the largest twenty-first-century strike years, but also the most cross-sectional in terms of industry representation seen in quite some time.

"Strike waves," as they are often called, are precipitated by incendiary triggers. These triggers may bubble below the surface until they reach a boiling point that demands attention. The 2020–2021 period saw one such breaking point with a number of triggers, including a resurgent women's movement, a cry for improved LGBTQIA+ rights, the immigrant workers' movement, the increasing volume of conversations to halt climate change, and the rise of Black Lives Matter and accompanying conversations. These triggers, coupled with flat (or actually declining) wage growth, escalating inflation, and a global pandemic, made the breaking point seemed inevitable.

Responses to these grassroots initiatives are critical. Corporate response tends to vary widely, from nonresponse to crackdowns and everything in between, with attentive and engaged responses that demonstrate vulnerability, accountability, and *actual* action succeeding best. Corporate America also assumes that an apolitical response is a good response, but this isn't always the case—especially today, when 64 percent of consumers worldwide take companies' social or political positions into consideration when making purchasing decisions.[7]

Public Relations Activities

The slimiest and most unproductive of today's DEI initiatives is public relations activities. They really shouldn't even be called DEI initiatives, but many organizations earn praise for the equality of their workplace through these initiatives.

◾

Most of us are well aware of the 2017 Pepsi commercial featuring Kendall Jenner handing a can of soda to a police officer. In the background are protesters with generic signage and overwhelmingly positive demeanors. The police officer accepts the can with a smile, and the commercial ends on a celebratory note. But the reality is, protests look nothing like that, and police brutality is more rampant than ever. This tone-deaf commercial attempting to celebrate unity and understanding became a pop culture meme, a stand-in for everything wrong with the way we understand current social justice initiatives.

◾

What many people don't realize or fail to appreciate is that commercials and PR moves like the Pepsi commercial are oftentimes just that—moves. Corporations are quick to align themselves with social initiatives while faltering in promoting DEI within their own organizations. JPMorgan Chase announced a $30 billion commitment to racial equality in the same year that accusations of racism in Private Client accounts were published in the *New York Times*.[8] Google announced the lackluster results of the investigation into firing Timnit Gebru and fired another team member from the AI team, both during Black History Month.[9] Quicken Loans is headquartered in Detroit, the Blackest city in America; meanwhile, the @blackatquickenloans Instagram account highlights countless stories of exclusion and discrimination within company walls.

◾

When company PR initiatives don't align with what's actually going on within the organization, the mistrust grows not only with consumers but also with employees (especially because employees can see behind the proverbial curtain). Company culture suffers, retention becomes increasingly difficult, and recruitment is nearly impossible. These PR initiatives serve to further isolate the workforce that the company has hired for the express purpose of bolstering its numbers of underrepresented employees. Even worse, many underrepresented employees cannot afford to leave a toxic company, or are worried about leaving the company too soon and having to explain their short tenure in a future interview, so they stay, trapped in the toxic culture behind the smokescreen of magnificently crafted PR.

▦

So how do we fix the DEI issues in Corporate America when we're relying on work that is sixty-plus years old and only taking action to stanch the flow of discrimination litigation and present a squeaky-clean image instead of actually driving toward a more inclusive workplace?

TWO

Does Diversity Training Actually Impact Inclusive Behaviors?

Corporate America's attempts at DEI have a far more negative impact than just failing to create an equitable workplace. In some cases, they actually create more discrimination than before.

The Impact of One Man's Memo

Take the now-infamous James Damore Google memo of 2017 as an example. I remember this memo so clearly, as it was published during the same time frame that I was negotiating my own offer to come work at Google. The title of this memo was "Google's Ideological Echo Chamber," and it specifically talks about Google's culture and diversity policies. Damore was self-prompted to write this memo because of a diversity training he attended, at the end of which the facilitators requested feedback.[1] The memo was his response to that call to action.

The memo, still available online today, is a ten-page manifesto of sorts which argues that differences between men and women in the workplace are "natural" and can be correlated to inherent biological differences. Damore goes on to argue that we cannot claim that disparities between opportunities and outcomes are attributable to oppression and that "reverse discrimination" (favoring underrepresented groups over the majority group) is an authoritarian way of trying to correct for these disparities. One of the most damning lines of the memo indicates that a critical difference between men and women is that women are more prone to neuroticism.

Perhaps even more terrifying than Damore and his memo was the internal mailing lists and forums that published their support for Damore's positions. Google's attempts to create a culture where employees had the freedom to speak up about anything and everything had gone too far: it was open season on diversity and inclusion efforts.

The Damore memo is not an isolated incident, either at Google or in Corporate America as a whole. The reality is that "diversity training" or "unconscious bias sessions" don't do what they are meant to. According to researchers at Harvard, "Short-term educational interventions in general do not change people," pointing to workplace safety training as another example of how one single session will not enact lasting workplace change.[2] Although diversity training may change how employees feel, it will not change the way they act. A number of studies show that individuals will frequently or even routinely discriminate against others without feeling bias or ill will, which leads us to the corporate culture issues of today—for example, an individual publishing a memo that blatantly discriminates against a group of employees on the basis of their identity.

The Code of Conduct Caveat

Diversity training is often the "first line of defense" for further explaining language found within a company's code of conduct. This code of conduct may include language such as the following. (All sample language has been pulled from Society for Human Resource Management policy document templates.)

> We all deserve to work in an environment where we are treated with dignity and respect. [Company Name] is committed to creating such an environment because it brings out the full potential in each of us, which, in turn, contributes directly to our business success. We cannot afford to let anyone's talents go to waste.

At the same time, it is common for the code of conduct to also include language around communications standards or "bringing your whole self to work," which might read as follows:

> At [Company Name] everyone should feel comfortable to speak his or her mind, particularly with respect to ethics concerns. Managers have a responsibility to create an open and supportive environment where employees feel comfortable raising such questions. We all benefit tremendously when employees exercise their power to prevent mistakes or wrongdoing by asking the right questions at the right times.

Instead of specifically defining issues such as diversity, equity, and inclusion within the code of conduct, this language creates the expectation for *all* employees to be treated with dignity and respect and for *all* employees to bring their whole selves to work—including racist employees. It also doubles down on the prioritization of equity for the sole purpose of business outcomes (and extracting employees' maximum talents). As seen in the case of the Damore memo, some employees will use this intentionally vague language as a way to actually enable their exclusionary or discriminatory behaviors.

Current Diversity Training Priorities

In so many ways, the current diversity training offerings across all of Corporate America are largely reactionary. In the same way that sexual harassment trainings got a facelift after the rise of the #MeToo movement, diversity trainings seek to minimize or mitigate employer liability for a variety of negative actions, incidents, and outcomes in the workplace. Diversity training programs were largely created to boost awareness of diversity, understand how to appreciate differences between coworkers and colleagues, and identify methods for improved communication, thereby creating a more positive work environment. The problem is, that's not the actual current outcome. To put it plainly: diversity trainings primarily achieve only the goal of preventing the next big lawsuit; they do not actually ensure that every employee is treated with the respect that they have a right to within their workplace.

What Are the Current Definitions of DEI?

In order for us to be on the same page, let's consider these generally understood definitions. Today, "diversity" efforts actually break down into three parts—diversity, equity, and inclusion. For the purpose of corporate contexts, these three can be over-simply explained as follows:

Diversity is the practice hiring of a representative mix of individuals—for example, if 13.4 percent of America is Black, a workforce that is only 3–4 percent Black is not diverse.[3]

▣

Equity is the practice of creating an environment where everybody has the same opportunity to succeed. In corporate environments, this looks like accessibility, access to accommodations, and even the simple things, such as conference-room chairs that are comfortable for plus-size people too.

▣

Inclusion is the practice of creating an environment where all individuals are able to participate actively and derive comparable benefits—for example, does a corporation value women's voices as much as men's? Are intersectionally underrepresented individuals just as included as majority individuals?

▣

Some companies or communities also add **justice** to their DEI definition, renaming the acronym JEDI. In this context, justice is defined as a plan for social change that requires a strategy to redress historical violence, inequality, trauma, and the unjust treatment of groups.

▣

Please be aware that JEDI is increasingly considered an inappropriate acronym for this sort of work, considering the references to *Star Wars* and what it means to be a Jedi within that universe. (We should avoid assigning stereotypes from a consumer brand or fictionalized universe to real-world situations with real-world impacts.[4]) Instead, consider using DEIJ as your go-to initialism. However you write it, the inclusion of justice in your DEI work remains an important evolution of modern-day DEI.

What Current Diversity Training Misses

Current diversity training focuses on the individual employee, their behaviors, their actions, and their understanding of workplace dynamics. These trainings portray DEI as a task that every single person has an opportunity to contribute to. Although this is true, every employee should not bear the burden for DEI equally. For example:

◫

Managers bear a responsibility for the environment they cultivate within their team. We focus so often on individuals and their actions. When a manager and an underrepresented employee have a conflict, the conversation typically goes to HR, and the eventual outcome is frequently that the underrepresented employee chooses to leave that manager's team via an internal transfer, or to leave entirely. Rarely is the focus on *proactively* training managers on how to recover these relationships; instead the focus is on reactively coaching the manager for their behaviors. Managers bear a greater burden for DEI, as it is their job to understand their team, understand the company culture, and understand how the two can work together (and/or advocate for their employees when the two are in conflict).

◫

Organizational leaders bear a responsibility for the behavior they model and the actions behind their words. Functioning cumulatively here (i.e., leaders bear all responsibilities that managers do, *plus* the responsibilities outlined here), leaders are responsible for making sure that their words are more than just words. Committing to inclusive hiring is great, but if there is no action taken when managers refuse to consider external candidates or make underrepresented candidates jump through additional hoops, that commitment falls flat. Similarly, when there are negative outcomes within an organization, leaders bear the responsibility to personally understand what went wrong and personally develop an organizational plan to create better outcomes in the future.

▣

Executives bear a responsibility to make DEI just as important as financial outcomes. DEI isn't just a nice-to-have. Quite simply, DEI represents the right for every employee to have a positive and *thriving* career within their place of work, without fear or stress or anxiety related to interactions that they have. DEI is just as important as the financial bottom line in the same way that having food to eat is equally important as having shelter to live in.

▣

In the drive to make the workplace a space where every single person can thrive, current diversity training leaves a vast chasm between what is possible and what is actually happening. James Damore felt emboldened to provide the feedback that led to his antidiversity memo. By contrast, I get nervous and sweaty, my hands metaphorically choking up, every time I write to my manager(s) or HR to give feedback on yet another gap I found in the training, for fear of them attributing my concerns to my identity, not to the marginalization the gap perpetuates. This contrast between our reactions plainly illustrates the damage that today's diversity trainings leave in their wake.

THREE

How Do We Measure "Diversity"?

When businesses think about DEI, the very first thought is *What is the financial gain from this activity?* as is the case for nearly every corporate initiative. The problem is, that kind of thinking is rooted in white supremacy.

◼

Using a business case to justify diversity initiatives is a tenet of white supremacy culture—always focusing on using revenue to motivate companies to do the right thing. In fact, white supremacy culture permeates many of the ways that we measure representation in the workplace. Consider organizations that

- ▶ Consistently assume that the goal is to grow—taking on more clients, serving more customers, and adding more staff, regardless of how well the organization can support the growth. Growth focuses on revenue even at the cost of the humans who drive the organization's production.
- ▶ Value production over process, even when that production is to the detriment of employees. Consider warehouses with

    items-per-hour targets that don't allow for bathroom breaks or food, ignoring the harm that this does to employees' bodies.

- ▸ Hold quantitative metrics as more important than qualitative ones. This almost always means money over community, but can also mean units sold or people in attendance instead of impact to the community or growth in morale.
- ▸ Prioritize short-term gains over long-term development. We see this often in response to community events—diving in to tweet in support of George Floyd and then failing to even acknowledge Black History Month the following year, for example.

Each and every one of these actions center whiteness and white supremacy, creating an environment that is built to fail underrepresented identities. Unfortunately, all four of these actions are very common talking points that companies today use to report on their progress.

OKR

The most common metric considered in Corporate America is OKR—objectives and key results. OKRs are often set at the executive level and then cascade down into business units and individual teams, becoming more and more specific the lower the management tier. In recent years, OKRs for diversity have often looked like increasing representation in hiring, increasing transparency both internally and externally, creating relationships with identity-based professional organizations, and increasing the diversity "slate" (or set of candidates) considered for leadership-level job searches.

▣

OKRs have their benefits, in that it's easy to assimilate new employees into the performance management structure, as the benchmarks are already cascaded in a formulaic and consistent way. However, they also have their downsides. OKRs require a ruthless practice of prioritization, such that not everything a company dreams of being able to accomplish in a year will actually be accomplished, or even see progress made.

▣

In order to prove value to shareholders and the public, companies often prioritize financial OKRs over all others. These can include a certain percentage of year-over-year sales growth, an increase in profitability, or a reduction of unnecessary expenses. Prioritizing such metrics doesn't leave a lot of room for diversity to have an impact, as employees often end up burned out before they have time to dedicate themselves to diversity. Not to mention, diversity's impact on financial metrics is a long game, not something that can be reported in the same quarter or the next.

Human Resource Metrics

There are some hard and soft human resource metrics that can speak to DEI improvements within the workplace. These metrics are a step in the right direction, as they center the person and not the business (although all of these metrics impact the business in some way).

▣

Job satisfaction is a measure of how happy an employee is in their current role. There are a number of factors within job satisfaction that tie into DEI in the workplace, including satisfaction with pay, with the role itself, and with the workplace environment. Comparing job pay satisfaction across demographic factors can illuminate wage gaps triggered by secondary factors*; comparing role satisfaction can illuminate ways to better align employees' responsibilities. Workplace environment satisfaction can be an indicator of strong relationships with coworkers or an inclusive environment that allows individuals to thrive.

▣

*On its face, your company may not have a wage gap; in other words, all new grad employees are paid the same, all employees that are middle managers are paid the same, and so on. However, secondary metrics might reveal a different story. If time to promotion or median performance rating varies by demographic factor, your workplace may not be set up to allow all employees to thrive. In failing to create this environment, you're triggering a pay gap by a different name. If each promotion takes underrepresented groups six or twelve additional months to achieve, the delta in pay during that time is your pay gap.

▣

Job retention is a measure of whether or not employees choose to stay at a company long term. Although in general, job retention has decreased in duration over the past few decades, there are still benchmarks to consider. If your employee turnover is high among underrepresented groups, especially in the first year or eighteen months of employment, you might have an inclusion problem. Take a closer look not only at the turnover rate but also the demographics—if the majority of your turnover comes from underrepresented groups, that might point to a problem with the culture or concerns with manager–employee relationships.

▣

Diversity by level might be the most commonly discussed soft metric for DEI. If there's no representation in senior leadership and executive roles, there is a massive DEI problem. If all of your underrepresented employees are in warehouse or data-center roles, the culture of the company is only allowing upward mobility for certain groups. Further, it is important to consider the number not just of women in leadership but also of underrepresented identities such as race/ethnicity or sexuality in leadership. The number of women in leadership has grown in the past decade (although this metric still needs work), but prioritizing the growth of other underrepresented identities in leadership is critical as well.

▣

Applicants versus employees is a final metric that helps indicate the growth potential for DEI within your organization. If there is strong representation in the applicant pool, but that representation sharply drops off for onsite interviews or new hires, this might indicate a bias or inclusion problem within the hiring process. If the applicant pool is devoid of underrepresented candidates, this might indicate issues with the way that the company speaks publicly about careers, culture, and personal development. These numbers should also continue to trend positively. Pay attention to when they begin to decline and understand what that change might be correlated to, such as a senior leader's disparaging comments or a failure to stand up for human rights.

Public Accountability

Many companies today publish annual diversity reports, whether as a part of their own corporate social responsibility efforts or in response to the 2020 Pull Up for Change social media campaign that demanded transparency on diversity in corporate workforces. While the more public visibility of these numbers is a fantastic change, reading through these reports truly highlights the fallacy that America's corporate workforce is getting more diverse.

▣

The reality is that women's participation in the workforce has dropped below 50 percent (down from 80-plus percent in 2010).[1] Still today, men are twice as likely to be hired, regardless of the hiring manager's gender.[2] Only 1 percent of Fortune 500 companies have Black CEOs, and only 3.2 percent of those same companies release race and gender data.[3] And things are only getting worse.

▣

Corporate America (and America as a whole) is becoming increasingly diverse. Millennials and Gen Zers are the most diverse generations ever.[4] We are less than twenty years away from America being a "majority-minority" country, and in less than ten years, white non-Hispanic people will barely be the majority at 55.8 percent.[5]

▣

Despite this, the deprioritization of DEI allows companies to disclaim responsibility for making meaningful progress. It also places the burden of making DEI-related moves in the workplace on the shoulders of underrepresented employees. The cycle of deprioritization perpetuates the existing inequity and bias in Corporate America and increases discrimination concerns through a lack of meaningful progress on equity in the workplace. The leaders responsible for this work struggle too, largely due to being set up to fail. In fact, there is significantly higher turnover in diversity-focused roles, such as chief diversity officer, than in other C-suite roles such as CEO.[6] Where else is high turnover in a C-suite role considered "the norm" and not something worth correcting?

So What Metrics Do We Use?

The answer is that we have to find the middle ground to get everyone on board. Centering metrics on financial outcomes is absolutely the worst way to go, but there are some people who won't be on board unless there is a financial outcome. Rather than changing the person, reframe your desired outcome through a lens they will understand while still naming the issue with tying DEI work to financial outcomes.

At the same time, DEI really doesn't productively move based on those financial metrics; it moves based on the human resource metrics and public accountability that we've discussed here. Merge all of these metrics into a narrative that makes sense for your organization—we'll discuss how in a later chapter.

| PART II |

A Change in Perspective

FOUR

Modern-Day DEI and Why Things Are Changing

As "corporate social justice" continues to evolve beyond sensitivity training and move toward true equity, it makes sense that corporate DEI would need to change as well. This shift, coupled with a more vocal workforce thanks to the collective bargaining and brain-trust capabilities of social media, has moved the power from the corporation to the people. Yet some companies still resist evolving toward a more modern understanding and execution of DEI.

How Powerful Is Social Media in Changing DEI in Corporate America?

Social media has given much more power to the individual than has ever been seen before. In the past five years, we've seen powerful campaigns changing the conversation, such as a viral spreadsheet of journalism salaries to enable women to gut-check their pay, and numerous employee bases such as Everlane and Alphabet using social media to self-organize unions and massive campaigns around issues in their workplaces.[1]

□

The impact of these social media campaigns is felt far beyond the thinly veiled corporate attempts at empathy of a PR office's coordinated response. Boycott campaigns, concerted recommendations of alternative businesses, and even advertising blackouts such as the Facebook boycott make the financial implications of social media–powered DEI campaigns something that companies need to plan for.

□

The combination of a pivot in what "diversity" actually means and the vastly strengthened ability of employees to communicate and collaborate outside of work has changed the landscape of modern DEI. It's no longer a nice-to-have for forward-thinking workplaces, but instead a must-have for a modern-day corporate workforce.

How Deep Does the Poorly Executed DEI Problem Go, and What Needs to Be Changed?

No longer stuck to the sensitivity trainings of the past, diversity in this modern execution actually comprises four layers, as explained by Edward Hubbard:[2]

► Workforce diversity: group and situational identities (race, gender, ethnicity)
► Behavioral diversity: work, thinking, and learning styles (beliefs and values)
► Structural diversity: different cultures, communities, and hierarchies
► Business diversity: markets, processes, creativity, and project management styles

Most companies think they have **workforce diversity** down—through employee resource groups, mandatory diversity and harassment training, comprehensive inclusive hiring policies, and corporate codes of conduct. As we've already discussed, these are not enough to adequately cover workforce diversity, but the bigger concern in this modern era are the remaining three layers, which are often ignored entirely.

▫

Behavioral diversity only changes through a top-down overhaul of the way a company thinks and operates. This is done in a very elementary way, through identifying and acknowledging unconscious bias, reevaluating corporate values to align with this new normal, and genuinely modeling a culture of inclusion at all levels of the organization. To further develop behavioral diversity, companies should look to the HR department (and likely an outside consultant) to further identify ways to bring inclusion and parity to these styles. For example: open-concept office spaces are not inclusive for those with ADHD. Does the company offer single-person huddle rooms for getting work done, or provide all employees with noise-canceling headphones that they are actually encouraged to use?

▪

Structural diversity is a little more complicated and might even be a little more painful to implement. Innovation cannot come without ensuring that all voices are in the room, including underrepresented ones. Evaluating the company hierarchy for gaps in representation and then making meaningful changes to equalize that representation are critical first steps. Global or multinational organizations also need to consider and be aware of the different corporate cultures of each region in which they operate. Are expats equipped with the tools they need to succeed in their new assignment?

▪

Business diversity is a strategic responsibility of the executive team. Are developing markets receiving the same investment as mature ones? Do the office locations in satellite cities have access to the same resources that exist at corporate headquarters? Does the company offer access to a variety of tools, enabling individuals to work in the way that helps them function best? (This is also behavioral diversity, but provision of resources is often considered financially first and then by their inclusion impact second.) Do corporate processes enable access and equity for all employees? Note that business diversity isn't talking about profit but about investment.

▦

All of these layers of diversity require a level of rigor and planning that is unlikely to currently exist within many organizations. Even if it does, these processes may only be reevaluated on a biannual (or even more infrequent) basis. Considering the DEI ramifications of each of these levels of business operations is critical to ensuring an equitable culture for the entire organization.

How Do We Currently Support DEI?

Today, DEI is largely the responsibility of the underrepresented communities themselves, and not by choice. You can still count the number of Black Fortune 500 CEOs on one hand—there are four.[3] Most underrepresented people in the C-suite are chief diversity officers, a role created to "deal with the growing DEI issue." This lack of meaningful representation in the highest corporate echelons means that there are very few marginalized individuals making decisions for how their marginalized peers should be treated at work.

▦

Diversity work largely falls to the HR department (if formalized) or to an employee resource group (if not formalized). In some companies, there is a separate office of diversity, but that office is still often tied to financial goals rather than to humanity goals. But in most companies, the same department that is responsible for firing you or putting you on a performance improvement plan is also responsible for making sure you feel safe, respected, and advocated for. Talk about a mind fuck.

▣

Within the HR department, there are a number of priorities, many of which are directly tied to performance reviews and bonuses. These might include hiring goals, HR case resolution, compensation planning, performance management, career planning, employee rewards systems, and succession planning. All of these functions impact the bottom line of the company, from having the right people in the right place to making sure payroll and budget even out. With all these competing priorities, how is DEI supposed to get the attention it needs?

How Does DEI Begin to Change?

In addition to the four layers of diversity, there are also four levels to DEI change, a model that was created in the 1970s but has continued to evolve to its current state.[4] These four levels apply to most workplace-related topics that require a human change. They are the personal, interpersonal, systemic, and cultural. You'll note that systemic is on this list *before* cultural, which is different than what you experience in US society today, where cultural change comes before systemic change. That order needs to be reversed too, but that topic is a whole separate book.

▣

Personal change refers to individual responsibility. Each of us has blind spots and ways that we are personally culpable for exclusionary and/or racist behavior toward others. By turning inward and reflecting on our own behaviors and biases, we can begin to grow. This work takes setting aside ego, committing time and energy to looking inwards and identifying a plan for relearning what DEI is and how we treat others.

⬛

Interpersonal change refers to the way we engage with others on a micro level. This includes single interactions with strangers, ongoing conversations with coworkers, the way we communicate and express ourselves, the language we use to describe others, and more. Interpersonal change requires taking an active step forward—this can look like allyship, creating or holding space, or elevating the voices of others.

⬛

Systemic change refers to evaluating the entire system. Nearly every system we use today was built on biased and discriminatory foundations, from banking to transportation to home buying and everything in between. The same goes for the way that our companies were built. Policies and procedures were created through the lens of founders' biases or industry convention. Business leaders must evaluate each system and identify the biases and ways that these systems disadvantage employees (and users/customers). Correcting these issues is the only way to provide a strong foundation for a company to move forward; shallow DEI efforts built on top of structural and systemic bias and discrimination do not improve workplace inclusion—they harm it further.

⬛

Cultural change refers to the permeation of all the other levels into the entirety of the workplace culture. These changes have to become the bedrock of workplace culture, the expectation for the way that we interact with one another. Business leaders must model and truly believe in these behaviors at their core and hold their teams accountable to do the same. Inconsistent culture, biased enforcement of policies or procedures, or pockets of the company where discrimination continues to fester will all lead to the failure of cultural change. It is the responsibility of every business leader to ensure that this change reaches all corners of the organization.

Who Is Helping Drive the Change?

Millennials are working their way into middle management and in some cases beginning to take on executive roles, as they have represented the majority of the US labor force since 2016.[5] Gen Zers are taking on demonstrably visible roles in the workplace, too. Take Zaria Parvez (Duolingo's social media manager) as an example.

▣

If you happen to read the *Harvard Business Review*, it recently published a piece titled "Stop Telling Women They Have Imposter Syndrome." The gist of the article is that imposter syndrome is not due to individual error or lack of confidence but to racism and misogyny. I read that article and was like, *um, DUH!* But not everyone would agree. In Corporate America, changes to DEI efforts largely rely on "group consensus" or leadership buy-in, which often means they're YEARS behind where popular culture is. But studies like this being published in academic sources give us content to rely on when having these conversations.

▣

Those same companies waiting for a consensus from leadership truly believe that "DEI will come in due time." Although this is true because of the demographics of rising generations and the US is less than a decade away from being barely a majority-white country, that's not a reason to wait for diversity to come. Diversity, equity, and inclusion don't happen because you want them to. They happen because you change what isn't working and listen to those not being heard.

Xennials and Gen Zers are also permeating corporate culture in a way that cannot be ignored, centered around three specific areas:

Compensation. Whereas Millennials and prior generations have been anywhere from slightly cagey to downright secretive around discussions of pay and benefits, Gen Z is all about transparency. This will impact not only the hiring process over the next couple decades but also DEI through increased awareness of wage gaps and inequity in pay for the same work and skillset. (Not to mention, studies show that Gen Zers value salary less than every other generation when making career decisions.)

Corporate social responsibility. If Millennials were the driving force behind the introduction of corporate social responsibility as a powerful PR and hiring tool, Gen Zers are tripling down on this as a priority.[6] Actions speak louder than words, and Gen Zers grew up with social media, meaning that they're shrewd enough to see through a black square on an Instagram feed with nothing else to back it up.

Diversity. In terms of not only diversity of identity but also diversity of thought and workstyle, Gen Zers are shifting the way we think about corporate culture. This generation grew up with technology in their hands and in their classrooms. To expect that a 9-to-5 desk job will work for them is to invite disaster.

The impact of focus on these three areas will require corporations to shift their priorities. Many companies already attempt to be competitive when it comes to compensation, but often lack transparency. They might have corporate social responsibility initiatives in place, but those are often shallow and lacking in diversity. To continue to attract top talent, corporations must maintain a focus on these three areas through the specific lenses that Xennials and Gen Zers care about.

Food for Thought

It is important to understand and acknowledge that there are organizations that are resistant to change, content with the way things are run, or convinced that their way is the best, most efficient, most profitable way. It might be the most profitable way, sure, but it is also likely that the system is benefiting from the exploitation of someone somewhere within that system. Leadership teams must examine this profit and break down the unsustainable corners it exists in to achieve a lasting and meaningful impact.

This sort of change is bold. It takes someone brave to stand up and challenge the status quo. But oftentimes, leaders are hesitant to do this. They benefit from the dysfunction and the way things are currently. Those record profits we've seen over the past couple years? That's led to record wealth growth too, mostly for the 1 percent. Why would leaders change a system that serves them so well? You wouldn't cut off the hand that was feeding you, would you?

But it's those leaders who are willing to be bold that stand to gain the most. These new systems, built on foundations that put humans first, people over profits? They're systems that are built to last. If you are a leader in your company and you've made it this far and are feeling a little shocked—consider how your employees feel. There are employees within your organization *right now* who have been advocating for *decades* for some of the changes we'll discuss in this book. They've fought tirelessly for a better workplace environment where everyone is respected and nobody has to suffer at work—and more often than not, they've been fired or have suffered other harms for speaking up.

▣

Furthermore, I think it's safe to assume that most of us believe slavery is over in the US, right? Emancipation happened ages ago, didn't it? I encourage you to overturn that notion and recognize the places within your own life where you are benefiting from the exploitation of others, then consider what that would look like when magnified to a corporate scale. Although this book is not about the carceral system, consider the prison labor that may create some of the goods you consume. Visit slaveryfootprint.org and answer eleven questions about your life to understand the impact of modern-day slavery on the way you live. When you get your result, multiply that by the number of employees in your organization. What's the impact of just *one* company's work-force on the number of others who are exploited for our gain and comfort?

▣

Today's supply chain enslaves more people than at any time in human history, and without systemic change, we cannot escape our influence on these practices. If you as a leader aren't willing to speak up about DEI for fear of the financial ramifications, surely the idea that today's consumer goods market is carried by the largest labor force of enslaved individuals that has ever existed is motivation enough to stand up.

FIVE

DEI Failures

Despite the PR campaigns, Black and Brown faces in marketing materials, and quippy social media accounts, Corporate America largely still "doesn't get it" when it comes to DEI.

Corporate Responses to DEI

In response to the murder of George Floyd, Mark Zuckerburg posted on Facebook: "To help in this fight, I know Facebook needs to do more to support equality and safety." He promised millions in investment to racial justice groups, even committing money from his own private philanthropy to the work. However, as is the case in much of the tech industry, Black individuals make up less than 4 percent of Facebook's workforce, and during an annual meeting just days before Zuckerburg posted that message on Facebook, executive leadership opposed an investor vote in favor of a resolution calling for a breakdown of its median pay gaps by gender and race. This is a textbook example of going through the PR motions of responding to "social moments" but then failing underrepresented communities where it matters.

◼

JPMorgan Chase has commitments to and statements regarding diversity and inclusion on its main website, stating that "diversity is an imperative—and together, we are all accountable for our culture of respect and inclusion," including a $30 billion commitment to advance racial equality. At the same time, racism is integral to the US banking system, going back decades, and Chase is no exception. In December 2019, a bombshell article came out in the *New York Times* featuring firsthand recordings of employees discriminating against affluent Black customers trying to join the Private Client offering.[1]

◼

To drive this point home, we can also look to the pop culture example of the British Royal Family as Meghan and Harry moved to America. In a recent interview, Meghan and Harry shared about the discrepancy between outside perspective and inside reality within the family. Meghan's experience in the family is akin to being hired with the promise that the company is diverse and arriving to see that the culture is toxic and downright discriminatory.

◼

All three of these examples took place within the past two years, at the same time that the movement for DEI has been the loudest it has ever been. Yet companies (and the Royal Family) still struggle to change.

Personal Experiences with DEI

To humanize the importance of DEI a little further, let me share some examples from my own experiences in Corporate America. These examples are discrimination-lite, meaning that although they were deeply traumatic to me, they pale in comparison to what some of your coworkers go through on a daily basis. They are also examples of what it means to not embed DEI in every aspect of how a company functions.

The damage to a wide swath of a company's employee base is often irreparable.

My Weight

When I entered the corporate workforce, I weighed more than three hundred pounds. At my highest weight, I was over four hundred. There have been countless times in my life that I have been excluded from participating in basic work situations that most people never even think about, all because of my weight.

Pre-COVID, I cannot remember a *single* conference room chair that I was able to sit in completely comfortably. Many of my desk chairs never really accommodated my size correctly either. Think about that for a moment: average of eight hours of work a day, ideally averaging forty hours of work per week. Over a decade in the corporate workforce. Despite being uncomfortable that entire time I was still expected to produce the same amount of work as everyone else in order to get ahead.

In fact, it was COVID and working from home that even gave me the confidence to finally address the situation with a coworker or boss. In a video conference one day, the team was making jokes about how awesome it was to work from home in their pajamas or loungewear, and I kind of just blurted out "Yeah, and to sit in comfy chairs too!" Everyone on the call looked at me funny, so I explained. I still remember the looks on their faces when they realized that something as simple as a chair had the power to make someone's day wonderful or miserable. Now I know that a chair that makes me feel comfortable and able to focus is a workplace accommodation at some companies, but pre-COVID me had no idea that was even an option! The lack of general awareness of an employer's accommodation resources makes life difficult for so many employees.

◦

Living in a big city has some amazing advantages and incredible positive notes. For me, living in a city made hanging out with coworkers and bosses a living hell. If an office building I worked in was a reasonable walking distance from a restaurant, it was commonplace for happy hours, lunches, or even the occasional meeting to take place at said restaurant. However, my mobility at the time didn't allow me to walk more than a block or two without being in pain, short of breath, or both. These casual encounters with coworkers became some of the most expensive days at my job, both financially and emotionally. I would make an excuse to stay behind as everyone left to start walking, then I would call an Uber and ride to the restaurant. I'd stay for the meal and typically be one of the first to leave so that I could Uber back either to the office or home, depending on the time of day. A free lunch on the company's dime for my coworkers became a $20 minimum expense (if there wasn't surge pricing!) that definitely wasn't reimbursable for me. Never mind if that outing was at a restaurant where the only option was a booth. Booths are a plus-size gal's fiercest enemy, and forcing someone to squeeze into a booth alongside coworkers after telling a white lie to avoid walking to the restaurant is a special kind of hell. I'm not advocating for never going out to eat—but choosing the restaurant across the street versus a few blocks away would be a more inclusive choice (and not just for plus-size folks like me but also for those with disabilities or children to get home to).

◦

If all that wasn't bad enough—have you ever paid attention to how companies talk about weight? Did you know that weight loss is the number-one most financially incentivized (or penalized) personal metric at work (closely followed by smoking cessation)? Many companies tie weight loss to lower insurance premiums or insurance rebates, or host weight-loss competitions (such as "dieting for dollars") provided by outside vendors.[2] In fact, more than one employer I have worked for has offered a "wellness club" that is actually a weight-loss program disguised as a "healthy living" community. These programs are full of embarrassment-inducing employee activities such as "physical wellness bingo" and BMI exercises, even offering Weight Watchers as a "self-care" resource. These same employers often have impossibly high standards to get approved for bariatric surgery, one of the best medical tools related to obesity.[3] Why are employers policing weight to begin with?

◙

Seventy percent of American women are size 14 or larger,[4] yet I was a willfully excluded minority in my workplace.

My Sexuality

Throughout my decade-plus in Corporate America, one thing that has been consistent is that I've been out of the closet as queer. However, despite coming out at the tender age of thirteen, I still have had to come out over and over and over again at every new job, because coworkers make the snap visual judgment that I am a white straight woman. If I've entered a job while in a relationship with a male-presenting individual, this personal share has been met with even more confusion.

◙

Despite this, my white straight passing privilege gives me tremendous freedom at work. I have never been (to my knowledge) looked on negatively for participating in an LGBTQIA+ employee resource group, attending Pride on behalf of an employer, or participating in a number of community-related activities. I've represented a former employer at a Human Rights Campaign gala and had the privilege of traveling abroad as an LGBTQIA+ representative of another employer. In other words, I am *very* out at work.

▣

Unfortunately, white straight passing privilege still doesn't shield someone from LGBTQIA+-related harassment or ignorance. In the span of a single week, a past coworker both asked me to educate him about LGBTQIA+ terms because he is "not well versed with gender queer and transsexual identities" and "voluntold" a teammate who is LGBTQIA+ to give a presentation about "what a great ally they are," completely invalidating their LGBTQIA+ identity and essentially forcing them to come out *again*. This former coworker was a manager and has been through a number of inclusive-workforce trainings both as an individual contributor and as a manager. HR's response to this situation was barely a slap on the wrist.

▣

In a former workplace of mine, I was in a position of authority and often worked the overnight shift. On the eight-hour overnight shift, there were occasions when I was the only female-identifying individual on the schedule. This was another workplace where I was out at work and my then girlfriend lived in the same town and frequented this workplace often. Unfortunately, this willing and unavoidable openness about my sexuality and how I identified positioned this information as a topic of conversation for employees. On one such overnight shift, a male employee who reported to me asked me repeatedly to give him advice on how to perform sexual activities on his female partner, as I "must be such an expert." I was unable to send the employee home, as overnight shifts are already a skeleton crew, yet I also was unable to get the employee to stop the unwanted conversation. The next day, I brought the situation to my manager. This employee was never talked to or written up for this situation as far as I am aware and continued to work for this employer (and on the overnight shift with me).

◻

Aside from my personal experiences, many organizations have inherently or subliminally anti-LGBTQIA+ policies, such as the following:

▶ Health insurance that leaves mental health costs disproportionately more expensive than other medical services (when homosexual individuals are twice as likely as heterosexual individuals to develop mental health concerns, with transgender individuals four times as likely[5]).

▶ Family planning services that cover what heterosexual families need but not all of what LGBTQIA+ families might need.

▶ Parental leave plans that do not provide equally for all possible parents and/or that treat adoptive parents differently.

▶ Benefits plans that make the inclusion of a same-sex partner unnecessarily complicated.

▶ Benefits plans that do not holistically cover the medical needs of transgender and nonbinary individuals.

▶ Any plans or policies that require a single long-term partner. (At one point or another, 20 percent of people in the US have tried polyamory, and 4–5 percent, or 17.5 million Americans, actively practice ethical nonmonogamy.[6] Although polyamory does not necessarily fall under the LGBTQIA+ umbrella, LGBTQIA+ individuals are more likely to be polyamorous.[7])

These policies add an additional layer of stress and worry to LGBTQIA+ individuals' workdays, further burdening their ability to perform to expectations, when they are already starting behind others.

My Mental Health

I was recently diagnosed with ADHD. This should have come as no surprise to me, as each of my biological siblings have similar diagnoses, but I was never tested. The diagnosis was a relief, as I finally had an explanation for different behaviors and struggles I had to deal with. Navigating ADHD in the workplace isn't quite as easy or relieving.

Many (in fact, almost all) American workplaces have a subsection of their HR team dedicated to accommodations. Essentially, an accommodation is an adjustment to the way you work that takes your physical or mental health, disability, or other need into consideration. For example, deaf employees may be provided with a sign language interpreter. The Americans with Disabilities Act includes ADHD as a recognized disability, and talking with my therapist and medical provider illuminated some things I was covering up with "executive functioning" that, with some new tools and resources, I might be able to let go of and make my day-to-day work life less stressful.

I applied for and received an accommodation related to different aspects of my ADHD. However, the process of applying for this accommodation involved jumping through a number of hoops. I already had documentation of an ADHD diagnosis, and my employer-sponsored health insurance was paying for both my therapy and my ADHD medication. Self-serve accommodations such as noise-canceling headphones were available without approval or a doctor's note, but more specific or nuanced accommodations required more information. The process required an appointment with my medical provider, a note from my therapist (to take to my medical provider), and then time of my own to submit the forms. In other words, to receive customized accommodations at work, I needed to pay the cost of an additional doctor's office visit (roughly $180).

▥

The actual legal requirement to receive an accommodation is to submit a request in plain language that outlines your suggested adjustments, equipment, changes, or other needs. Next, the requester and the employer interactively determine appropriate accommodations and then activate those accommodations. So long as the changes or modifications do not cause "undue hardship," the employer must comply. The added requirement of a doctor's note, therapist information, and other documentation was initiated by the employer and not mandated by the Americans with Disabilities Act or other governing policies. As a friend of mine recently joked, "I don't need a doctor's note to tell me that a flexible 9–5 schedule and a certain way of taking notes will set my employee up for success."

▥

Further, ADA compliance doesn't necessarily immediately create an inclusive working environment for those who are granted accommodations. Oftentimes, there is ambiguity around what is considered a "reasonable request," and an employee has to "shoot their shot" to see if their accommodation will get approved, thereby disclosing an unnamed condition that requires an accommodation. Next, if a company grants the accommodation but the company culture is not conducive to the accommodation, oftentimes implementation will fall by the wayside. For example—as in that "9–5" joke, if an employee is granted a flexible schedule but company culture generally demands extended hours to meet goals, an employee will often be pressured into ignoring their accommodation for the sake of performance, promotions, bonuses, and raises. Finally, adherence to accommodations is not necessarily a metric that managers are commonly evaluated against, providing no external incentive for managers to prioritize accommodations, especially if they are "inconvenient."

The Duality of DEI at Work

The harmful duality of DEI and discrimination isn't always something that a law or company protects us from encountering. Oftentimes, legalized discrimination is taking place within companies that are receiving tremendous credit for their inclusion activities. This duality causes some of the most harmful experiences in the workplace, often because there isn't anyone invested in preventing them from happening. These completely legal situations include the following:

> During a job interview, a colleague of mine was explicitly told by a mentor not to wear their wedding ring or reference their same-sex partner in the conversation, because the hiring manager was openly anti-LGBTQIA+. The hiring manager discussed their own opposite-sex partner at length during the interview conversation.
>
> When in a sales meeting with a company whose CEO was anti-LGBTQIA+, a coworker told a friend of mine to "not push your gay agenda." This friend rarely talked about their personal life, but the mere presence of the reality of their personal life was taken as a threat to the CEO's worldview.
>
> When preparing for a sales meeting with a massive $6B company, I was informed that the dress code for male employees at this company was shirt and tie, nothing more specific. The dress code for women had a list of ten or more requirements, including pantyhose if wearing a skirt, shirts that did not show the collarbones/clavicle, and a number of other archaic requests. As the only woman from my company attending the meeting, I was required to

comply, despite not being an employee, due to the size of the company's account with my own employer.

Although attendance was not explicitly required at many happy hours I have attended in my career, the impact of not attending and/or not drinking prevented career advancement at a rate equal to those who did consistently attend due to the relationships and other connections those at the happy hours had access to.

A start-up considered itself "pro-diversity" and openly interested in hiring neurodiverse individuals, not for inclusion reasons, but because "autistic people are [stereotypically] good at" the open roles the company had listed. When the hired individuals did not fit the stereotype, the company "managed them out" of the organization.

It is common for marginalized individuals to experience open discrimination against certain hairstyles or textures as a part of a dress code or unspoken requirement or expectation. (Only twelve US states currently outlaw discrimination based on hair texture.) The lack of consistent protection in these policies is a form of ongoing legalized harm.

This legal discrimination also includes inconsistent application of DEI efforts across identitics. Did you know that even though 90 percent of US-based companies claim to prioritize diversity, only 4 percent consider disability as part of those initiatives?[8] Failing to consider disability as a part of DEI initiatives not only harms the individuals who do not have access to resources that fall under the company's DEI umbrella but harms every employee.

Your Coworkers' Experiences

As I mentioned at the start of this section, each of these experiences individually is an example of discrimination-lite. I've still received promotions and raises at work and have still largely loved my job(s) despite these experiences. But each individual DEI failure adds up, and over time they overwhelm the spirit, doubly so for intersectionally marginalized individuals.

▣

Our coworkers face DEI failures far more severe—outright racism and homophobia, rising anti-Semitism and Islamophobia, ongoing sexual harassment that is *just* below the bar that qualifies it for an HR investigation (or does rise to the bar, but the perpetrator gets paid millions to quietly leave the company), and so much more. Reading these stories may make you want to ask your coworkers whether they've had similar experiences. *Don't.* That's called trauma porn—being fascinated or intrigued by someone else's misfortune. Instead, assume that stories like these and far worse exist in your own workplace. Assume that there are entrenched barriers to everyone having an equitable experience at work. Then fight to change that.

SIX

The Impact of COVID-19 on Corporate Diversity

In many ways, COVID-19 and its side effects and correlated impacts changed the landscape and raised the bar on what qualifies as meaningful corporate diversity moving forward.

▣

The loudest change came in the form of the **largest racial reckoning in modern-day history**. Cities across America and countries around the globe advocated for the critical importance of Black lives in a way we've never seen before. Specifically in Corporate America, employees got creative, holding Venmo drives online and using their corporate matching donation benefits to double and triple donations to racial equality organizations. The way companies showed up mattered too. Did companies share a position on the events of summer 2020, and did evidence show that they treat their Black and Brown employees equitably too?

▣

A much quieter but equally powerful change came as a result of **mass work from home**. Employees with disabilities have begged for years to have the ability to work from home (WFH). Some employees have written petitions or proposals; others have tried to gain access to WFH opportunities through doctors' notes or mental health provider advocacy. The answer, in many cases, has been a blanket "It's not possible" or "You won't be as effective from home." And yet in 2020, the entire world's base of "knowledge workers" (defined simply as those who do their work from a computer) largely (and relatively easily) transitioned to WFH. Some companies gave up their office spaces in major cities, and other companies have announced permanent WFH offerings, signaling that WFH can be and is profitable. It took the entire world being shut down for some corporations to realize that the accommodations their disabled employees had been asking for actually worked just fine.

Finally, we saw the introduction of a **two-class environment** at many companies. The aforementioned knowledge workers were able to work from home five days a week, whereas the "frontline workers"—clerks, stockists, warehouse employees, and so on—still had to show up in person and punch a clock. The impact of this was disproportionately felt by Black and Brown communities, further exacerbating the delta in equity in much of Corporate America.

All three of these massive reckonings have forever changed the way we think about DEI in America. Platitudes and soft-footed plans for future change won't cut it anymore; employees feel more empowered than ever to use their voice. From the Amazon workers who protested lack of COVID protections to the advocacy for Juneteenth to be a national holiday, a new day is here.

Racial Reckoning and Social Movements

Beyond a willingness to speak up and an emboldened set of possibilities for organizing and demanding change, a variety of social movements have begun or grown bigger in an effort to drive an understanding of the lack of equity in the workplace and beyond.

■

The Fight for $15 is a movement that began in 2012 when a handful of fast-food workers went on strike in New York City, and today is partnering with congresspeople and global organizations to advocate for a fair living wage.

■

The Google Walkouts in 2018 saw more than twenty thousand Google employees walk out to protest sexual harassment and misconduct, as well as the way that Google handles sexual assault cases.[1]

■

Everlane's customer experience team pushed to unionize for better working conditions in the middle of COVID-19 and then saw the team gutted by layoffs in the middle of that push.[2] Everlane and other brands have seen employees leverage Twitter to build unions over the past couple of years.

■

Pull Up for Change was a social movement that began in 2020 to push brands beyond performative social media posts in response to the murders of George Floyd, Ahmaud Arbery, and Breonna Taylor. The movement called on brands to share the racial/ethnic makeup of their employee base, explicitly excluding field/retail store/customer service employees (where racial/ethnic minorities are often concentrated). The goal of the movement was to encourage brands to have at least 10 percent Black corporate employment—equal to the percentage of Black college degree holders.[3]

▣

The Make It Black campaign, which launched in 2021, seeks to shift brands away from performative Black History Month advertising. The initial partnership is with beauty brands to execute campaigns shifting perceptions around what it means to be Black, and the gross profits will go to a fund to give capital and grants to Black-owned businesses and founders.

▣

Parallel to COVID, the impacts of a number of mass-casualty events have forced companies to face the inequitable situations they have created. Amazon's response to the tornadoes that swept the lower Midwest in late 2021, crushing Amazon warehouses and killing employees who should have been at home, is a microcosm of the larger labor issues that have been brought to the center of public discourse.

▣

These and other movements are forcing companies to take a closer look at the way they handle DEI issues, as modern communication platforms enable public accountability. But is public accountability enough?

The Impact of Mass Work from Home

As a result of COVID, hundreds of thousands of knowledge workers suddenly found themselves working from home for a couple of weeks, which became a couple of months, which then evolved into more than two years and counting. This mass shift to WFH for knowledge workers had a profound impact on the immediate contexts of work as well as the long-term ramifications of corporate decisions and what we include in the scope of DEI.

◫

In the near term, mass WFH began to prove wrong the notion that productivity diminished when employees were not colocated side by side in cubicles. Over the past two years, despite a global pandemic, many businesses who rely on knowledge workers have posted record financial gains. A mid-COVID study found that 60 percent of workers felt more productive at home than they thought they would be.[4] This accidental and supposedly temporary shift accelerated a debate that has plagued modern workplaces—why *not* work from home? From 16 percent of the US workforce working from home in 2019 to 71 percent in December 2020, what was once a fringe benefit or a rare exception for certain employees is now largely the norm.

◫

The problem with WFH is that it shined a spotlight on a previous inequity that now has no excuse for existing. Disabled workers have long asked for fully remote work. Single parents have had to negotiate the 3 p.m. pickup with their boss's expectations. Those with ADHD have had to navigate overwhelmingly distracting open–floor plan workplaces when they had a perfectly good desk at home. Furthermore, individuals who did get approved for remote work faced other challenges—access to leadership, advancement opportunities, raises, equitable benefits, and more. Pre-COVID, the prevailing belief was that these were one-off cases (they weren't) and that individuals were simply grateful to have a job with that kind of flexibility (yes, but they deserve respect and career progression too). Now, more people are aware of this disparity; it's not hidden anymore.

◫

Take the example of these two employees:

◫

Employee 1 is a marketing employee working out of an employer's office in Los Angeles, making $75,000 per year; they also occasionally work from home. **Employee 2** is a marketing employee working remotely for the same employer in a neighborhood of Seattle, also making $75,000 per year. Both employees are single with no children or pets, and this is their first corporate job.

◫

Both employees receive the same health care benefits, same 401k 6 percent contribution and 3 percent match, same internet reimbursement, same home office setup stipend. The cost of living in Los Angeles is moderately comparable to that in Seattle—as of this writing, the median rent differs by $100, and the median home price differs by $1,000. Financially, these employees are on similar ground on the first day of their employment.

◫

However, because remote work is deprioritized and often demonized, and because companies still rely on "visible production" as a metric for employee productivity, over time, Employee 1's advantage grows. After eighteen months of employment, Employee 1 is promoted and receives a 6 percent raise, now making $79,500 annually. Employee 2 receives a good performance review, but isn't promoted. The gap begins to widen as Employee 1 now contributes an additional $405 annually to their retirement fund (including employer match), among other changes. Assuming for the sake of this example that neither employee ever receives another promotion, but does receive modest annual raises of 3 percent, Employee 1 retires at a significant advantage. That $405 annually will grow into thousands of dollars at retirement that Employee 2 will never see. Employee 1's base salary for annual raises is larger than Employee 2's, so their wage growth over time will also vary by thousands of dollars.

▣

This example only highlights the financial disparities when we prioritize in-office work and demonize remote work. Denying remote work also cuts off access to broader and more diverse talent pipelines and prohibits many people with disabilities and caregiver responsibilities from having access to "knowledge worker" jobs. As we saw with the pandemic, when remote work becomes a priority, it works better too. We compressed more than a decade of remote work innovation into less than a year, and we now have access to a number of tools enabling us to do our best work at home more easily than ever before.

Two-Class Environments

The introduction of a two-class environment at work did not begin with COVID, but it certainly gained national attention, and not for good reasons. While knowledge workers (including myself, to be clear) holed up in their homes and worked from home, feeling a more limited impact to their health and finances in the early days of COVID, frontline workers did not have that luxury.

▣

In fact, workers who just days before COVID were considered disposable, or even third-class citizens, became the most critical component of society's ability to function during lockdown and the days that followed. Doordashers and UberEats drivers, Instacart delivery people, and all those who worked any other courier service were suddenly risking their lives to enable others to stay safe in their homes. Grocery clerks and stockists, warehouse employees, medical workers, and more became the cogs in the machine that kept society from devolving into absolute mayhem.

▣

I was living with someone as the world began to lock down in early 2020, and the disparity in our lives was made painfully evident as we shared a home. I woke up, walked ten feet to the bathroom, twenty feet to the kitchen, and the same thirty feet back to my desk, and didn't leave the apartment for days on end. I had our groceries delivered via Amazon Fresh, ordered almost every basic necessity online for two-day delivery from stores such as Target and Costco, and never once missed a paycheck or feared furlough. The person I was living with was furloughed nearly immediately and pivoted to delivering groceries via Shipt. They were gone eight to twelve hours a day delivering groceries from various stores all over the Chicago suburbs, coming into contact with hundreds of different people every day. They came home exhausted, worried about exposure, and too tired to do anything else, but needing to get up the next day to do it all again in order to pay the bills.

▣

This two-class environment remains today, as many knowledge workers saw their 401ks increase, stock investments boom, and general financial situation hold steady (or even improve) throughout the course of the pandemic, while many frontline workers have new debts to pay, months of lost paychecks to make up for, and in many cases, long-haul COVID symptoms to deal with.

SEVEN

The Language of Inclusion

DEI has expanded beyond just a training or a checkbox and is now embedded in the way we treat and view individuals, the way it should have been all along. This evolution, coupled with a more vocal workforce thanks to the collective bargaining and brain-trust capabilities of social media, has created tremendous new ways of communicating about equity.

▣

With this increase in communication also comes an increase in the nuance of language. As I come to understand my own identities further, and even as I was doing research for this book, it struck me how *academic* DEIJ work has become. We talk about the "pedagogy of the oppressed" (the title of an actual book I recommend in the resources section) and a number of topics defined by ten- and twenty-dollar phrases. We look at literature reviews, created through the academic gaze, and fail to consider that access to academic opportunities is a privilege in and of itself. If someone with a doctorate degree finds this work to be overwhelmingly academic, how do we expect someone who is still learning what DEIJ stands for to feel?

Take this debate as an example: Do we identify as latine, latinx, latina, or some other word altogether? I've been doing a lot of research on latine versus latinx since beginning this book, and the answer is no more clear to me now than it was a year ago. Spanish is not the Indigenous language of Central and South America, so the claim that white people are colonizing the Spanish language with *latinx* is . . . impossible? Spanish IS the language of colonizers, so really *latine/latinx* is like a reclamation of identity, right? *Latine* is the Spanish-inspired version of *latinx*, so latine might feel more natural to some. Both of these words might leave out Portuguese speakers in Brazil, who might prefer something else entirely. You see now why I fumble with what word to use.

But this brings us to a larger point—so many people who *want* to be more inclusive at work are scared to try, because we've packed inclusion full of fancy language (see: the list of words on the cover of this book). What if we broke down some of these words, used approachable language, and centered actual equity in this work instead of getting overwhelmed by academic definitions of the factors that contribute to and detract from DEIJ?

You don't need to understand words like *pedagogy* or *oppression*, *decolonize* or *diaspora*, *marginalized* or *multicultural competency* in order to work toward a more equitable (and less checkbox-focused) workplace. These words are important, yes, as they define different experiences, sources of strife, and desired outcomes of DEIJ work. But to get started, it's really most important that you understand your privilege (access based on your identity), your bias (automatic prejudices you hold internally), and what you can do to break those down. The rest will come.

EIGHT

The Underrepresented Advocacy Experience

Underrepresented individuals often unfairly shoulder a more significant amount of the burden for changing corporate environments. This starts as advocating for community issues and ends with underrepresented individuals leading committees, educating senior leaders, or even holding the role of chief diversity officer, hoping and praying for influential sponsorship to enact corporate change.

⊞

The term *invisible labor* has long been used to describe unrecognized work in a corporate environment. Examples include the work women do in being inordinately responsible for office social events and celebrating important milestones, as well as the work underrepresented identities have to do in educating their coworkers or leaders.

⊞

The responsibility falling on minority shoulders is nothing new—it's often a result of companies seeking knee-jerk solutions to PR crises in times of company or cultural upheaval. When the events of 2020 took place, between racist language around COVID-19 and the murders of Breonna Taylor, George Floyd, and others, companies leaned on employees from those identity groups to lead the response, often without first checking in to see how they were doing.

▣

The outcome, unfortunately, is a negative impact on regular performance. In fact, because diversity initiatives are seen as extracurricular activities, they often are the first thing to go if an employee's core role performance is suffering. Even if performance isn't an issue, if leaders haven't bought in on the importance of DEI work, employees don't get due credit for their labor. Even if leaders have bought in, credit isn't guaranteed.

▣

Employee resource groups, diversity committees, and anecdotal conversations also aren't going to get to the root of Corporate America's DEI problem. Nor are ERGs going to fix the underrepresentation of women and minorities in executive leadership positions. The outcome is shallow diversity efforts meant to provide legal liability disclaimers (as was the case in the 2011 Supreme Court case in which the presence of an antidiscrimination policy was enough to prove that Walmart hadn't been discriminatory).[1]

▣

Meaningful change will come only when companies take on DEI initiatives as a central imperative, not as an extracurricular nice-to-have.

A Matter of Perspective

A few years ago, I was working on my own performance review. I had to capture all the things that I had accomplished over the duration of the review time period and clearly articulate my contributions to the company. My regular role's metrics were all on target; none of them were particularly earth shattering, but I hadn't missed any targets either. My DEI work, by contrast, was truly incredible.

◻

A mentor who helped me document my performance noted that my contributions to our company's DEI initiatives were well above what was expected of someone at my job level. They hoped that this performance would be accurately reflected in the evaluation my manager would give me. The following is a sampling of my contributions:

▶ Leading a committee comprising people managers in DEI efforts to improve our department, while being an individual contributor myself

▶ Leading a company-wide project on DEI that required interfacing with senior leaders and "making the case" for the initiatives that we wanted to implement

▶ Driving accountability for a program designed to create changes in DEI for a company-wide program

I finished documenting my performance for that cycle and shared the information with my manager. Despite DEI being a "strategic initiative" for that performance review period, I was evaluated as having met expectations for my role—nothing more, nothing less. Again, I met all of my regular role's targets and went above and beyond for DEI efforts (among other things), but was told only that I met expectations. As added salt in the wound, at that particular company, meeting your expectations does not make you eligible for a merit-based raise.

◻

The difference in perspective between my manager and my mentor (also a manager) highlights the degree of latitude in the valuing of DEI efforts within an organization. If you report to a manager who does not value DEI as a significant contributor to your role or your work, most organizations will not punish that manager for failing to recognize the DEI work.

The Labor of Representation

This failure to recognize the immense labor that goes into creating a more inclusive workplace further highlights companies' failure to prioritize DEI as a strategic imperative. This labor is necessary for underrepresented individuals to feel quasi-safe in their work environment, yet companies do not value the benefits that this (free) labor brings.

In fact, the work that ERGs complete on a volunteer basis would cost tens (if not hundreds) of thousands of dollars per year if completed by an outside consulting firm or by full-time employees dedicated solely to this work. Yet in providing these free services to the organization, ERG leaders and committee members help companies generate hundreds of thousands (if not millions) of dollars in revenue, at the cost of their own career and financial advancement.

| PART III |

Toward Human-Centric DEI

NINE

A Roadmap for Truly Effective Corporate DEI

After eight chapters of dissecting what's wrong, what does meaningful corporate DEI actually look like? How does a company set out on a path to be inclusive and equitable without seeming performative? The answer is simple, but the execution is much more complicated.

We live in a world where corporate DEI is no longer an option. It is an expectation, a baseline minimum, a signal that a company respects its employees. At the height of early COVID fear, George Floyd's murder became worldwide news as the spark that ignited a renewed chorus of voices for equity. The asks were not new. The ramifications were not new. What was new was the visibility and engagement with a global audience. That spark ignited the largest antiracism movement since the civil rights movement. The hesitantly hopeful wish after George Floyd's murder was that *this* would finally be the time something changed. This worldwide visibility, this level of engagement couldn't all be for naught, could it? Know that underrepresented people know better. The exhaustion weighs heavy. In the case of George Floyd, nine minutes and twenty-nine seconds of harm were captured on film, yet we weren't sure that the perpetrator would be convicted. In Corporate America, a different kind of uncertain death to the soul is the same.

Put the Human First

Above all else, any DEI strategy needs to put the human first. If you've read all the horror stories and truly awful moments in this book or in Corporate America news in general, you know this to be the case. If your company's motivation for prioritizing DEI is the financial and innovation gains that the organization believes will follow, **STOP**. Your employees are not here to carry the company's financial growth on their back while not being respected, being abused and degraded at work, and being seen as subhuman.

⬚

Company leadership makes a number of assumptions when an employee walks in the front door of a company:

- ▶ That they will prioritize the company while within the walls of the office
- ▶ That they are leaving all personal baggage at the door
- ▶ That they are grateful for the compensation they receive
- ▶ That the compensation they receive provides them financial security

These assumptions are accompanied by many others, all of which also disregard the whole human. The reality couldn't be further from these assumptions. Many employees walk through the front door carrying the weight of their family or household on their shoulders. Many employees are not paid enough (see: gender pay gap, racial pay gap, lack of universal living wage, and many other topics this book does not have the space to cover). Many employees cannot use their full wage at their discretion, as they are responsible for the basic necessities and/or financial obligations of others.

■

Not putting the human first ignores all of these considerations. Prioritizing the business over the human is the reason the term *human capital* exists,[1] as though employees' only value to the company is their production output, not their individuality, creativity, and humanity. Before a company, or you as a leader, can even begin the true work of creating an equitable workplace, you must first evaluate whether or not employees are treated like the *human beings* they are.

Once You've Centered the Human

Once it is clear that humanity and basic decency are the first priority, a company can proceed. DEI initiatives deserve the same **strategic thought, intentionality, future planning, and humble listening** that every other component of the business receives. If planning for next year's sales quotas and forecasting is a month-long project requiring approvals all the way up to the VP of sales, DEI deserves that same attention and rigor. To enable this, leadership buy-in is necessary. (And in an ideal world, approval for diversity initiatives starts at the top.)

■

The "right" DEI solution will vary company by company; the only wrong answer is to fail to prioritize it. But a DEI initiative centered in these four components will advance meaningful equity for underrepresented employees that matters far more than a public relations move. The next four chapters will delve further into the four components.

TEN

Intentional

Centering DEI work in strategic thought, intentionality, and future planning provides a runway for this work to receive equal respect compared to other organizational initiatives.

■

It is common for DEI work (and goals) to be planned by leadership or employee committees, often starting fresh each year. This creates a model wherein quarter 1 is spent discussing and deciding on initiatives, quarter 2 is spent getting executive buy-in, quarter 3 is spent planning and preparing to execute, and quarter 4 is spent executing, only to start over again in quarter 1 of the following year. This model allows only a painfully short time for the actual execution of work while also spending an immense amount of time in the planning stage. Inverting this model with multiyear planning up front and a broader commitment to overall DEI work enables more time during each individual year to be spent on taking action.

Consider the following companies:

COMPANY A—ANNUAL DEI PLANNING

Year 1 Q1—Decide on annual initiatives with an employee committee

Year 1 Q2—Secure executive buy-in

Year 1 Q3—Prepare to execute annual initiatives

Year 1 Q4—Activate annual initiatives

Year 2 Q1—Decide on *new* annual initiatives

Year 2 Q2—Secure executive buy-in

. . . and the cycle continues.

COMPANY B—MULTIYEAR DEI PLANNING

Year 1 Q1—Decide on multiyear plan and define metrics for success with C-suite leadership

Year 1 Q2—Break multiyear plan into annual segments and create plans for each segment

Year 1 Q3—Prepare to execute annual initiatives

Year 1 Q4—Activate annual initiatives

Year 2 Q1—Measure year 1 initiatives (one quarter of data) and launch year 2 initiatives

Year 2 Q2—Measure early success; identify opportunities to improve on year 2 initiatives

Although Company A and Company B spend the same amount of time (three quarters) planning, Company B is able to see more early (and lasting) success because it built more robust plans up front. In addition, due to the scope and commitments of the multiyear plans, C-suite leadership is more likely to be involved from the outset, minimizing time spent securing buy-in after initiatives are developed.

Choosing a Planning Style

There are advantages and disadvantages to each kind of planning (annual versus multiyear), but multiyear planning has some significant selling factors for DEI longevity. First, the longer timeline and higher-level visibility within the organization can lead to broader adoption of the plans. Perhaps more important, the nature of multiyear planning makes it easier to look toward lasting change rather than the topic of the moment.

* * *

For example—during the civil rights movement of 2020, many companies chose to take bold stands on matters of racial equity, policing, and where their corporate donation dollars went. Fast-forward to 2021. Many of those same companies were silent on matters of racial equity, except perhaps during Black History Month or on Juneteenth. Annual DEI planning lends itself to the shifting topicality of the moment. Although this might seem to be a benefit, as flexibility in planning can lead to more empathetic responses, in most cases it leads to inconsistency and ends up doing more harm than good to the communities it seeks to impact.

* * *

Multiyear planning would prioritize racial equity and other topics that the company is invested in more comprehensively. This leads to a more consistent and sustainable position that the impacted communities can actually rely on, creating meaningful change in and outside the company.

A Note on Executive Buy-In

Much of what is discussed in this book hinges on executive buy-in. Organization-wide changes often require executive sponsorship, or specific budgets, or both. Finding allies on the executive team is critical to the success of nearly any DEI strategy. Existing allies for new initiatives might be found in the executive sponsors of ERGs or other identity- or community-based groups.

▣

If you are in an executive role yourself, note that you bear a greater responsibility to advocate for and initiate change within your organization, primarily due to the authority and influence you hold. The higher up in an organization you are, the more visible you are as well. The impact of your sponsorship or backing can stretch far beyond the single initiative or plan you are supporting—it can be seen as a vote of confidence that underrepresented communities really do belong at your organization.

Moments versus Conversations

Our gut response to a call for DEI is often to center our efforts on events—spotlighting LGBTQIA+ individuals during Pride Month, Black individuals during Black History Month, and so on. Perhaps we host special talks and invite individuals from those identity groups when it is "their turn" for celebration. Perhaps our social media content focuses on these identity groups, and our charitable contributions support relevant identity-specific organizations. These efforts are all well and good, but they miss two major inflection points that could truly change the course of your DEI efforts.

Create Consistent Visibility

Communities are often busier than ever during moments of community celebration and do not have the bandwidth or energy to participate in yet another event. Event-specific activities are far less impactful than an overall improvement to the culture of DEI within the organization. If we are trying to amplify underrepresented voices, we can't do it by holding a conversation once a year and/or when there's already visibility (e.g., during Pride Month).

·

When we reach out to a community and seek to amplify their voices when they are already in the spotlight, we're actually not doing anything for them at all. In fact, we are instead benefiting ourselves from the spotlight they have momentarily extended to us as well.

All Community Engagement Must Center Community Needs First

Our efforts to uplift communities often center our own needs first— whether through PR, corporate DEI metrics, or some other business-centric priority. All community engagement must center community needs first, must be empathetic, and must first seek to build a relationship and trust before engaging in transactional requests. (Ideally, no element of the relationship is transactional.) To achieve this, we must engage in one-on-one conversations with ERG leadership teams and always lead with "How can we support you?" Engagement should be an offering of support and resources, not an insertion into the community's existing programming, creating net-new content, and so on. Engagement also should not be at the last minute (e.g., two weeks before the start of Hispanic Heritage Month); these relationships should be built for the long term.

·

Many ERGs are already creating year-round programming that supports their community-specific needs and goals. Rather than creating fresh content at a corporate level, engage with the ERGs and champion or spotlight the work that they are already doing. Take responsibility to proactively identify ERG programming calendars and offer resources to bolster their efforts. Engage with the ERG and ask members what would be most helpful—answers will vary by group.

▣

When doing ERG outreach to engage in corporate events or initiatives, consider that not everybody feels the same way about participating. Instead, approach ERGs from a place of giving: "We have these resources available, and we'd like to give them to you."

▣

Finally, most ERGs are hesitant to engage in corporate-level initiatives because they are well aware that the company stands to gain more than they do. Issues around rapport building and trust also exist for these groups, primarily due to being steamrolled and not listened to. All engagements should begin with relationship building before all else.

Targeting Specific Communities Can Actually Further the Harm

Targeting specific communities will almost always create a conversation about whom you are leaving out and whom you are including, and what your motivations might be. It is a commonly held yet often unspoken belief that by increasing representation or opportunity for one minority group, we are absolved of needing to increase representation of others. This could not be further from the truth.

▣

As an example, there are thousands of companies that offer a military/veteran/teacher/first responder discount to members of the community. These discounts are a wonderful way to give back and thank these community members. However, these companies often don't put the same energy into programming or opportunities for all underrepresented groups. If these companies do choose to offer a program targeting one underrepresented group, they're likely to be getting DEI "PR cred," but they might actually be promoting resentment between underrepresented groups. Differential recognition is a reminder that we often have to fight one another for scraps because most places don't create enough "value" to go around.

Build in the Order That Matters

We previously talked about the levels of DEI change—personal, interpersonal, systemic, and cultural. These levels apply to the intentional way that we approach DEI changes within our organizations too. And as an ever-present reminder, DEI efforts should focus on lifting up *all underrepresented identities* while also being mindful that by focusing broadly, DEI efforts will inherently privilege those with greater social power. Balancing broad initiatives with targeted community engagement will create lasting impact.

Intentional DEI efforts should first focus on the individual level and should prioritize those already in the organization. Work to understand (if you don't already) the climate within your organization for different underrepresented groups. Identify the ways in which corporate policy, behavior, and norms contribute to the climate and how those factors can be changed. Don't place the burden of these discoveries on the underrepresented groups themselves, either. Do the work, be introspective, and try to identify what your organization is doing to harm its employees.

DEI efforts should then turn toward the interpersonal. If you have a record of HR cases, review them. How often did interpersonal conflicts alleging discrimination receive a slap on the wrist when more attention should have been given? What sorts of employee dynamics led to interpersonal conflicts? Are there teams or departments where certain environments persist more than others? Seek out these trends and identify what is causing them, then work toward a solution.

▣

Only when both the personal and interpersonal levels have been thoroughly evaluated and worked on, opportunities for improvement identified, and actions toward resolution begun will it be time to move on to systemic and cultural change.

Inclusion Is Rarely Convenient

Inclusion (or lack thereof) isn't always obvious. Take Clubhouse, for example. Clubhouse is a free social media app that is somewhere between live radio and livestreaming that seemingly anyone can join. However, at its inception, it was audio-only, with no option to access transcriptions or closed captions, or to chat in any way. It was also launched Ivy-League-Supper-Club style, by invitation only. Those are two pretty big barriers to inclusion. Despite this, there are many individuals who are fiercely passionate about DEI who still are leveraging Clubhouse because we sometimes (actually oftentimes) forget about inclusion on the basis of things other than race. (In response to growing public pressure, Clubhouse did recently add captioning, although the app remains far from wholly inclusive.)

▣

Inclusion isn't always convenient but it's a company responsibility to do it anyway. As an oft-marginalized person, it feels lonely to see everyone flocking to the new shiny social media and wanting to join yourself but being unable to. If you're passionate about or an advocate of DEI, or frankly just a decent human being, you should want to engage on platforms where all the members of your audience can be in community with you. This includes the way a company approaches marketing, the way it engages with its employees, and nearly every other opportunity for conversation that exists in the corporate space.

■

Having the "choice" to be inclusive is a privilege. If inclusion isn't your first thought when you check out a new platform, it means that you are, in some way, not from a group that is inherently unable to use the platform fully. This shows up in many different forms—those with disabilities being nervous about conferences or audio-only apps, those who are plus size being nervous about boarding a plane, those who are Black being downright terrified of getting pulled over—those who don't align with the mentioned category may not have the same fears in the same scenario. Create a method to evaluate every element of your business for inclusion in a way that checks your blind spots too.

ELEVEN

Thoughtful

DEI should never be started in response to a social movement. A company's first or loudest attempt at inclusion should not be a blacked-out square posted on Instagram in support of Black Lives Matter. DEI requires a meaningful audit of existing-state issues in the organization: what's the current pay gap, how much of the current employee base is made up of underrepresented identities, is there representation in key leadership roles, what supplier guidelines are in place, and other key measures of meaningful diversity. The gaps revealed by the audit provide places to take action first, before anyone sends out signal-boosting messages of equity outside of the workplace.

How Reactionary DEI Fails: An Example

As a queer person, when June 1st rolls around, I want to mute all of my social media, if only to avoid the advertisements from every single consumer goods company pushing its "pride collection." It happens every year like clockwork, and every year companies trot out the same tired, often repeated merchandise splashed in rainbows. Even worse, sometimes the pride collection is just existing goods packaged together to fit the narrative. A seven-pack of socks, one pair in each color of the rainbow? Groundbreaking.

◼

First of all—I know this is sacrilege, but . . . I actually don't like rainbows that much. I'm not alone, either. There are cottagecore lesbians, Wild-fang queers, and dozens of other categories of LGBTQIA+ individuals who typically wouldn't be caught dead in or around a rainbow. Oftentimes these collections are tacky, splashing a rainbow on things we wouldn't normally wear or buy anyway, or are "disposable consumables"—things we'll throw away after the Pride Parade. All the more reason to skip the rainbows.

◼

Second, the traditional ROY G. BIV rainbow doesn't actually include the whole LGBTQIA+ community. In recent years, the various flags and colors that represent the community have begun to evolve. Philadelphia created a version of the pride flag that factors in intersectionality. The Gay Progress flag captures a better cross section of the community and again highlights intersectionality. The 2018 new Pride flag includes not only the notes of intersectionality but also emphasizes the trans flag, elevating the trans community and recentering the history of trans people of color and their importance to the queer rights movement dating all the way back to the Stonewall riots.

◼

And finally—the biggest trend of them all is to change a company's flag to include a rainbow on social media for the month of June. The deepest irony of Pride Month is that these social media logos are displayed even by companies actively working against LGBTQIA+ rights. In fact, nine of the most LGBTQIA+-supportive companies from a PR perspective actually each gave $1 million or more to antigay politicians in the last election cycle.[1]

◼

As soon as June is over, the collections disappear (or hit the clearance rack and sell for $3 or less). Those Trevor Project donations get sent and then queer folks never hear from these companies again . . . until Pride Month the following year. These sorts of reactionary, trend-hopping, and poorly thought-out DEI initiatives harm the communities they seek to support, while companies get to cash in on the PR of faux community engagement.

Spotty Support Does More Harm Than Good

Perhaps worse than bandwagoning onto Pride Month is inconsistency. Posting a Black social media image in support of Black Lives Matter and then completely skipping Black History Month. Going all out on Martin Luther King Jr. day (and probably posting a JFK quote instead), but having to be educated on Juneteenth by the company's social media followers. Celebrating Latinx (or Hispanic) Heritage Month and leaving out Brazil, despite its also having gained independence in September.[2]

By not rooting DEI efforts in careful thought and consideration, these half-baked attempts to catch up to what peer-set companies are doing or to hop on a PR opportunity end up harming the brand in the eyes of underrepresented individuals. If a company had retention issues or cultural issues prior to these flubs, afterward things will only get worse.

Even the best-laid plans can get lost in the pitfalls and tropes of performative or ineffective DEI efforts. Avoiding these can enable your DEI efforts to have more lasting impact and positive outcomes not just for the community they target but also the organization.

The first, and perhaps most obvious, pitfall is engaging in conversations around diversity only when "culturally relevant." This might look like a black square Instagram post in support of George Floyd and BLM or changing your company logo to be rainbow-toned during Pride Month, but not doing much else to support DEI initiatives. The intent of these initiatives is to appear "plugged in" and "aligned" with the social movements of the moment without actually having to go any deeper. The outcome is that they appear shallow and end up doing more long-term harm than good for the organization.

A critical pitfall to avoid is treating all underrepresented groups the same. This can look like a mentoring program open to "all underrepresented identities," generally being in support of "diversity," or considering x percent total representation of all underrepresented identities sufficient in the hiring process. Operating this way ignores the nuances of each underrepresented group and its specific needs within your organization or industry. For example, within the tech industry, Asian+ representation is strong, whereas Black+ and Latinx+ representation has changed by less than a percentage point, and Native representation not at all, since 2014.[3] Meanwhile, disability representation is hardly measured at all.[4] At the same time, it's costing American companies $64 billion annually to replace employees who depart due to discrimination.[5] To treat all underrepresented groups the same would be to ignore the severe underrepresentation of some groups and the strong representation or "overrepresentation" of others.

Finally, a third pitfall that even companies entrenched in DEI work can fall into is not having all DEI efforts be congruent toward a singular goal of deeper inclusion and representation. Fragmented DEI efforts within a company often lead to resentment (due to lack of executive sponsorship), inaction (due to lack of oversight or measurement), or poor execution (due to less thoughtful planning). Effective DEI requires avoiding all three of the pitfalls I've described here.

What Do You Do Instead?

As much as it might be painful *not* to post when every company in your peer set is posting, truly engaging DEI efforts will speak volumes louder than any single social media post ever could. A few months before a heritage month, surprise your ERGs with additional funds to be used with no executive oversight on what it must be used for. Engage in community-specific financial giving built on relationships—for example, build a meaningful and nontransactional relationship with the Indigenous community that is native to the land your corporate headquarters is on. In Australia, New Zealand, and Canada, this is done every day with a "land acknowledgment" at the beginning of meetings, small gatherings, and even sporting events.[6]

TWELVE

Bold Leadership

DEI requires bold leadership. Messaging and action should signal that inclusion is a priority, leadership should have objectives directly correlated to advancing DEI, and members of the executive team should serve as sponsors for key initiatives. Leadership should also be modeling and truly invested in the behaviors that drive an inclusive culture. This investment from leadership communicates to the rest of the organization the importance of DEI values and the alignment of those values with the goals of the business.

◼

As we've acknowledged, there are organizations that are resistant to change, content with the way things run or convinced that their way is the best, most efficient, most profitable way. In order to drive change, leadership teams must unilaterally be committed to change and must be willing to tear the organization to the ground and root out those dark festering corners in order to achieve a lasting and meaningful impact.

◼

It takes bravery to stand up and challenge the status quo. Know that there are employees within your organization *right now* who have been advocating for *decades* for some of the changes we discuss in this book. They've fought tirelessly for a better workplace environment where everyone is respected and nobody has to suffer at work—and more often than not, they've been fired or have suffered other harms for speaking up, if they have even had the luxury of speaking up.

What Does Bold Leadership Look Like?

Most leadership books talk about bold leadership in terms of being courageous and willing to take risks, and prioritizing brilliant results over everything else. The first two qualities carry over to what we're talking about here. The third, not so much—unless the result is respect, not financial gains.

Bold leadership in the DEI space takes truly caring about the person above all else. As Corporate America is set up today, when we truly look at how things are being measured, the human is the least important entity. Bold leadership means putting the human first, prioritizing the relationship over the business. This requires courage and the willingness to take a risk, which also requires an understanding beyond corporate DEI talking points.

Bold leadership requires a universal absence of neutrality. Elie Wiesel wrote these words in his books *Night, Dawn,* and *The Accident. Night,* specifically, is a book about his experiences as a Jewish prisoner in the Auschwitz and Buchenwald concentration camps.

> We must take sides. Neutrality helps the oppressor, never the victim. Silence encourages the tormentor, never the tormented. Sometimes we must interfere. When human lives are endangered, when human dignity is in jeopardy, national

borders and sensitivities become irrelevant. Wherever men and women are persecuted because of their race, religion, or political views, that place must—at that moment— become the center of the universe.

Neutrality (or an abdication of a position) in matters as extreme as those we find in the world right now is an implicit cosigning to the oppressor's actions. Silence, whether literal or through lack of allyship, encourages the actions of those who would oppress others. To stay silent in your leadership, to remain neutral and attempt to please all sides, is not the answer.

Invest in Your Team So Others Don't Have To

After the events of the past few years, and considering America's history in general, racism and discrimination should no longer be a surprise to anyone. With this in mind, invest in your team up front. Engage in antiracist and antidiscrimination education for your team and your organization. Commit money, time, and energy on an ongoing basis and ensure that new team members get access to past training too. Offer educational content in different formats to engage everyone's learning style—offer courses or training, read books and conduct a book study or club, hire a DEI consultant, and offer any number of other opportunities to learn. This action should take place on a recurring basis and not just be a part of onboarding or annual compliance training, because DEI efforts must go far deeper than compliance. By providing your team and organization with a base level of information, you (we hope) save underrepresented individuals the burden of having to educate you. When mistakes are made, your team has this foundation to lean on and can respond in a more productive manner as well.

THIRTEEN

Acknowledge Your Mistakes

Acknowledging mistakes is critical. An inability to acknowledge mistakes will cause history and harm to repeat on a never-ending loop. And if you've done something wrong, learned why it was a problem, and do it again—that's no longer a mistake. That's active harm.

A Note on the "Devil's Advocate"

It is not uncommon to hear someone take up the point of the "devil's advocate" during many conversations on DEI topics. The point of this is to create an argument based in fact (or fiction but argued as fact) as a counterpoint to whatever content is being discussed. In many situations, the individual arguing this perspective believes it to be a logical comparison. In others, it is used to poke holes in a discussion.

▣

Although there are certainly times that a devil's advocate argument is good, such as during scientific research to consider the opposite outcome of a certain hypothesis, conversations on DEI topics are not the place. DEI work is rooted in lived experience—actual individuals' experiences with discrimination, oppression, racism, and other harmful actions. The ability to have a devil's advocate argument in a DEI space often speaks to the privilege of the person presenting the argument—to talk about oppression or discrimination as a "good" thing for the sake of a counterpoint speaks to the privilege of never having had to experience being on the receiving end.

There is nothing abstract about these experiences, nor is their harm up for debate. We all die eventually; immortality is not yet "a thing." Similarly, until we've ensured systemic equality, it is unlikely that systemic racism and other forms of discrimination and harassment will end.

Finally, the most simple definition of *devil's advocate* is to argue an opinion you do not agree with. Unfortunately in our current environment, many individuals argue the devil's advocate point while also truly believing in the argument they present. This is therefore no longer a devil's advocate argument, but instead simply bald-faced bigotry and a deeply harmful mistake.

What Acknowledging Your Mistakes *Shouldn't* Look Like

When I think about acknowledging mistakes, I think about highly publicized DEI blunders and how the individual or organization recovers from them. These conversations in the public space often serve as "call-ins," or opportunities to reflect on the way business is done versus how it *could* be done. These are different than "call-out" scenarios (equally necessary, but can lead to cancel culture—again, a whole separate book).

As a clarifying point—*calling out* is issuing a direct (and often public) challenge to an individual's words or behaviors. This is usually done with the intent of "exposing" their behavior to others. *Calling in* is discussing a problematic behavior with a peer by explaining the misstep with compassion and patience. Calling out is necessary to interrupt and prevent further harm—such as the intentional misuse of someone's pronouns. However, calling out can go too far—such as doxxing or engaging in crude vigilante justice. By prioritizing calling in within Corporate America, we are asking people to set aside their pride.

Let's for a moment consider the world of conferences. It's a story we've all seen before—white conference organizer hosts conference with majority-white speaker lineup and people feel left out, so they speak up. The difference in this case? It's not the conference organizer's first time being asked to bring forth more diversity.

▣

In 2016, a conference that was in its second or third year released its annual tentpole event lineup. In the posting of speakers on Instagram, one thing was glaringly obvious. Each of the twenty-six smiling faces in the carefully curated marketing graphic was white. After some community members and possible conference attendees spoke up, the conference organizers were quick to respond. They thanked those who spoke up for "sharing their heart," stated how much they valued the feedback, and encouraged community members to reach out directly to discuss the issue further.

▣

At face value, this response was perfect PR; the conference organizers couldn't have been coached any better. They didn't turn off Instagram comments, they didn't deny responsibility, they didn't dispute or defend. They really seemed to take the conversation to heart.

▣

A few days later, the conference responded in a new social media post, stating "We have never intentionally NOT invited women of color to participate on a higher level (as a panelist, speaker, etc.), however, we absolutely accept full responsibility and sincerely apologize for not being intentional about ensuring that our conference is as diverse as possible and that women of all colors, shapes and sizes are represented well." The post encouraged individuals to apply to be speakers for the following year's event. But the true harm was rooted in what was unspoken in this apology: they had personally reached out to speakers with whom they had relationships, or had received recommendations from lookalike peers—and built a speaker lineup that was largely devoid of true representation and inclusion. Not only had they *not* invited underrepresented individuals to participate (intentionally or otherwise), they *had* intentionally curated a speaker lineup comprising those whom they believed to be "quality" speakers. To hand-select a speaker lineup places the burden of representation on the organizer to proactively reach out to all qualified speakers.

▨

Community members weren't satisfied. The initial comments didn't ask for much other than a reflection on how this came to be the speaker lineup. The goal was basic inclusion—not above and beyond, just the bare minimum. **At this point, the right move (or at least a positive move) would have been for the organizers to step back, to engage in antiracist and DEI education for the team, to perhaps even put ticket sales or the official speaker lineup on hold, pending evaluation in a few weeks' time.** Instead, a few days later the organizers posted what seemed to be a second apology to the conference Instagram account. They promised an improvement in representation and that they would be taking some time to step back and evaluate how they were structuring the event. However, the event moved forward largely as-is, save for a few underrepresented speakers who were shoehorned into the existing lineup.

▨

Fast-forward four years later to pre-COVID 2020, and the speaker lineup for that year's conference went live online. Face after face of white speakers was eerily reminiscent of the situation four years prior, with underrepresented speakers barely scratching the surface of the full speaker list. The difference this time was that underrepresented community members felt brave enough to demand a change. Over the next few days, stories of discrimination beyond "just" the speaker lineup began to come out. To share a few:

- ▶ A deaf attendee was told that the conference could do anything *but* get her an interpreter to accommodate her attendance (when the cost of an interpreter would be less than 2 percent of total estimated revenue from ticket sales).
- ▶ A Jewish attendee was promised that the event was not religious, but then had to join in Christian prayer when two separate keynote speakers lead the entire conference in prayer during their keynotes.
- ▶ A talented Black designer applied to speak on more than one occasion through the form referenced in the original apology and via email, but never even heard back.

The conference organizers' response was nearly the same as the one four years prior, including some of the following statements:

- ▶ They had worked hard to build a conference community where all feel welcome while also providing top-quality content. (This is a classic subliminally racist comment correlating "white" with "quality.")
- ▶ They were open to learning more while also staying true to the community they were already building. (They are demonstrating unwillingness to diversify their community to reflect today's world.)

- ▶ They survey their past attendees to learn more about whom they want to see on stage the next year. (Building from past years already shown to have issues creates an insular community that further discriminates.)
- ▶ They want to have people resonate with the content and see people who look like them, but also need content to be in alignment with the brand and uphold their educational quality standards. (Again, they're saying that inclusion is not "on brand.")
- ▶ If people brought up their concerns in a "professional and open" way, they would be more willing to make changes. (Here, they are engaging in tone policing.)

Due to COVID, the 2020 conference was postponed. Despite this, we can take away some massive lessons in how we acknowledge our own DEI mistakes and failings.

What to Do Instead

Lead with Listening

Oftentimes in DEI scenarios, individuals are expressing how what you or the company did made them feel. Our feelings are individual and unique to each one of us. It is not our responsibility to correct or explain to someone else how they should feel. By leading with listening, we can understand what others value and how they want to feel, enabling us to modify our organization's actions to more closely align with their expectations.

▣

Listening requires setting aside ego. You've probably learned that there is a difference between hearing and listening—it is the latter that is truly critical here. Set aside your beliefs, your perspectives, and your assumptions, and truly listen to what the person has to say. Engage, ask questions, seek to learn from what they are sharing. Set aside the desire to make a devil's advocate point, and truly absorb what the individual is sharing. Pay attention to the boundaries that the individual sets as well—just because they are sharing their experience doesn't mean they are there to answer intimate identity-based questions. Treat the conversation as you would learning from a professor rather than as sparring with your favorite debate partner. (Trust me, I need to heed this paragraph as badly as anyone. Listening is not one of my best skills.)

Listening also requires a commitment to action. There is a difference between being physically present in a room or on a call while individuals share their experiences and actually engaging with the intent to take action. The individual doing the listening must also be doing their own separate work—they cannot expect to learn everything about a topic just from a conversation or two. Investing in outside training, consultants, books, and other materials accompany listening to firsthand experiences.

Speak Second

This goes hand in hand with listening, but seek to (1) speak second in every interaction with another person regarding a DEI failing and (2) pause before responding. We often only halfway listen to what others are saying because we're busy preparing a rebuttal in our heads. (Tell me it's not just me!) Pausing before responding gives our brain a few more seconds to more fully process what the other person has said. It also helps take the heat off of whatever we may respond with, turning that snarky sarcastic retort into a genuinely thoughtful contribution.

Own Your Privilege

Privilege is immutable. Your socioeconomic status, where you are from, where you live now, how hard you have worked—these things do not negate the access to privilege that white and white-presenting individuals have. Ever. This privilege shapes the way we move through the world, our experiences, what trauma we face, and how dangerous to our life and livelihood that trauma is. Owning this privilege and recognizing that you have a leg up will help you approach your mistakes with a more "eyes wide open" focus.

You're not always going to get it right. I don't either. I'm certain there are DEI-related mistakes even within the pages of this book. I learned and grew over the course of writing it and changed some of my advice here too. That's okay. What matters is how you react, how you respond, and whom you pull up alongside you.

Ending Checkbox Diversity Discussion Guide

Use this guide to kick-start a conversation about *Ending Checkbox Diversity*, but don't let it block the conversation—follow your thoughts.

- ▶ What part of *Ending Checkbox Diversity* made you feel the strongest emotion?
  - ▪ Why? Was it a positive or negative feeling?
- ▶ What made you pick up this book? Did you have that same intention after you finished it?
- ▶ Do your definitions of DEIJ vary from the ones presented herein? How so?
- ▶ Does your own organization prioritize DEIJ? If so, what does that look like? If not, what do you think is holding it back?
- ▶ What would your organization look like if it were more diverse and inclusive?
- ▶ Taking it one step further to our personal lives—what would your friend group look like if it were more diverse and inclusive?

▶ Do you have any biases or gaps in information that you want to explore further now?

▶ How do you think your own biases inform or influence the way you move through the world and interact with others?

▶ Where have you experienced the most resistance to DEIJ? How did you respond?

▶ What are some specific ways that you have advocated for change, and what are the successes and challenges you've faced?

  ▪ If you haven't previously advocated for change, do you feel more empowered to do so now? Why or why not?

Notes

Introduction

1. McCormick, K. "The Evolution of Workplace Diversity." *Houston Law* 2007: 11–14.

2. Crenshaw, K. W. "Framing Affirmative Action." *Michigan Law Review First Impressions* 105 (2007): 123. http://www.michiganlawreview.org /firstimpressions/vol105/crenshaw.pdf.

3. "Employment and Discrimination: Exploring the Climate of Workplace Discrimination from 1997 to 2018." *Paychex*, August 1, 2019. https://www.paychex.com/articles/human-resources/eeoc-workplace -discrimination-enforcement-and-litigation.

4. Jameel, M., and Yerardi, J. "Workplace Discrimination Is Illegal. But Our Data Shows It's Still a Huge Problem." *Vox*, February 28, 2019. https:// www.vox.com/policy-and-politics/2019/2/28/18241973/workplace -discrimination-cpi-investigation-eeoc.

5. Jackson, A. E. "New Study: 3 in 5 U.S. Employees Have Witnessed or Experienced Discrimination." *Glassdoor*, October 22, 2019. https:// www.glassdoor.com/blog/new-study-discrimination/.

6. Bleiweis, R. "Quick Facts about the Gender Wage Gap." Center for American Progress, March 24, 2020. https://www.americanprogress.org /article/quick-facts-gender-wage-gap/.

7. Lloyd, C. "One in Four Black Workers Report Discrimination at Work." Gallup, March 8, 2021. https://news.gallup.com/poll/328394/one -four-black-workers-report-discrimination-work.aspx.

8. Accenture. *Equality = Innovation: Getting to Equal 2019: Creating a Culture That Drives Innovation*, 2019. https://www.accenture.com /_acnmedia/thought-leadership-assets/pdf/accenture-equality-equals -innovation-gender-equality-research-report-iwd-2019.pdf.

9. Joy, L., Wagner, H. M., and Narayanan, S. *The Bottom Line: Corporate Performance and Women's Representation on Boards*. Catalyst, October 15, 2007. https://www.catalyst.org/research/the-bot tom-line-corporate-performance-and-womens-representation-on -boards/.

10. Hunt, V., Layton, D., and Prince, S. *Diversity Matters*. McKinsey & Company, 2015. https://www.mckinsey.com/business-functions/people -and-organizational-performance/our-insights/~/media/2497d4ae4b 534ee89d929cc6e3aea485.ashx.

11. Allen, B. J. "Diversity and Organizational Communication," *Journal of Applied Communication Research 23*, no. 2 (1995):143–55. doi:10 .1080/00909889509365420.

Chapter 1

1. Dobbin, F., and Kalev, A. "Why Diversity Programs Fail." *Harvard Business Review*, July–August 2016. https://hbr.org/2016/07/why-diver sity-programs-fail.

2. Santana, J. "How to Easily Beat and Survive the Coming Massive ERG Budget Cuts!" Linkedin, March 30, 2020. https://www.linkedin.com /pulse/how-you-can-successfully-fight-coming-ergbrg-budget-cuts -santana/.

3. Santana, "How to Easily Beat."

4. Nataroš, T. "Employee Activism: What It Is, Why It Happens, and How Companies Can Respond." FAMA, August 3, 2020. https://blog.fama .io/how-to-respond-to-employee-activism.

5. Peachey, R. "The 2020s: Decade of Employee Activism." *theHR-DIRECTOR*, February 19, 2020. https://www.thehrdirector.com/the -2020s-decade-of-employee-activism/.

6. Moody, K. "Upticks, Waves, and Social Upsurge." *Spectre*, November 15, 2021. https://spectrejournal.com/upticks-waves-and-social -upsurge/.

7. Kreuser, A. P. "Should Your Business Take a Political Stance? Here Are 3 Brands That Did—And How Their Customers Reacted." *Inc.*, September 27, 2019. https://www.inc.com/amanda-pressner-kreuser/should -your-business-take-a-political-stance-here-are-3-brands-that-did-and -how-their-customers-reacted.html.

8. Togoh, I. "JP Morgan Pledges $30 Billion to Help Remedy Racial Wealth Gap." *Forbes*, October 8, 2020. https://www.forbes.com/sites/isabeltogoh /2020/10/08/jp-morgan-pledges-30-billion-to-help-remedy-racial -wealth-gap/?sh=21bba588594d.

9. Clark, M., & Schiffer, Z. "After Firing a Top AI Ethicist, Google Is Changing Its Diversity and Research Policies." *The Verge*, February 19, 2021. https://www.theverge.com/2021/2/19/22291631/google-diversity -research-policy-changes-timnet-gebru-firing.

Chapter 2

1. Conger, K. "Exclusive: Here's the Full 10-Page Anti-Diversity Screed Circulating Internally at Google [Updated]." *Gizmodo*, August 5, 2017. https://gizmodo.com/exclusive-heres-the-full-10-page-anti-diversity -screed-1797564320.

2. Martin, M. "5 Reasons Diversity Training Usually Fails." *Fast Company*, August 3, 2020. https://www.fastcompany.com/90535289/5 -reasons-diversity-training-are-not-successful-as-anticipated.

3. US Census Bureau. "Quick Facts United States," 2019. https://www .census.gov/quickfacts/fact/table/US/PST045221.

4. Hammond, J. W. "Why the Term 'JEDI' Is Problematic for Describing Programs That Promote Justice, Equity, Diversity and Inclusion." *Scientific American*, September 23, 2021. https://www.scientificamerican .com/article/why-the-term-jedi-is-problematic-for-describing-programs -that-promote-justice-equity-diversity-and-inclusion/.

Chapter 3

1. International Labour Organization. *Gender Inequality and Women in the US Labor Force* (Geneva, Switzerland: International Labour Organization, 2020).

2. Reuben, E., Sapienza, P., and Zingales, L. "How Stereotypes Impair Women's Careers in Science." *Proceedings of the National Academy of Sciences 111*, no. 12 (2014): 4403–08. https://doi.org/10.1073/pnas.1314788111.

3. Donnelly, G. "Only 3% of Fortune 500 Companies Share Full Diversity Data." *Fortune*, June 15, 2017. https://fortune.com/2017/06/07/fortune-500-diversity/.

4. Fry, R., and Parker, K. "'Post-Millennial' Generation on Track to Be Most Diverse, Best-Educated." Pew Research Center, August 14, 2020. https://www.pewresearch.org/social-trends/2018/11/15/early-benchmarks-show-post-millennials-on-track-to-be-most-diverse-best-educated-generation-yet/.

5. Poston, D. L. "3 Ways That the U.S. Population Will Change over the Next Decade." *PBS NewsHour*, January 2, 2020. https://www.pbs.org/newshour/nation/3-ways-that-the-u-s-population-will-change-over-the-next-decade.

6. Cutter, C., and Weber, L. "Demand for Chief Diversity Officers Is High. So Is Turnover." *Wall Street Journal*, July 13, 2020. https://www.wsj.com/articles/demand-for-chief-diversity-officers-is-high-so-is-turnover-11594638000.

Chapter 4

1. Gerrit De Vynck, N. T. "Six Things to Know about the Latest Efforts to Bring Unions to Big Tech." *Washington Post*, January 26, 2021. https://www.washingtonpost.com/technology/2021/01/26/tech-unions-explainer/.

2. Hubbard, E. E. *How to Calculate Diversity Return on Investment* (Global Insights Pub., 2004).

3. Hancock, B. "Think Black CEOS Are Scarce? It's Worse Than You Think." McKinsey & Company, April 29, 2021. https://www.mckinsey .com/featured-insights/coronavirus-leading-through-the-crisis /charting-the-path-to-the-next-normal/think-black-ceos-are-scarce -its-worse-than-you-think.

4. Gardenswartz, L., and Rowe, A. *Diverse Teams at Work: Capitalizing on the Power of Diversity* (Alexandria, VA: Society for Human Resource Management, 2008).

5. Rogers, A. "How Gen Z Could Change Corporate Culture—and How We Can Keep Up." *Forbes*, October 1, 2019. https://www.forbes.com /sites/forbestechcouncil/2019/09/30/how-gen-z-could-change -corporate-culture-and-how-we-can-keep-up/?sh=7c7535cb64ca.

6. Mawhinney, T. "Understanding Generation Z in the Workplace." Deloitte, August 30, 2019. https://www2.deloitte.com/us/en/pages /consumer-business/articles/understanding-generation-z-in-the -workplace.html.

Chapter 5

1. Flitter, E. "This Is What Racism Sounds Like in the Banking Industry." *New York Times*, December 11, 2019. https://www.nytimes.com/2019 /12/11/business/jpmorgan-banking-racism.html.

2. Lewis, A., Khanna, V., and Montrose, S. "Employers Should Disband Employee Weight Control Programs." *American Journal of Managed Care* 21, no. 2 (February 1, 2015): e91–e94.

3. Belluz, J. "We're Barely Using the Best Tool We Have to Fight Obesity." *Vox*, December 7, 2017. https://www.vox.com/science-and-health /2017/12/7/16587316/bariatric-surgery-weight-loss-lap-band.

4. George-Parkin, H. "Size, by the Numbers." *Racked*, June 5, 2018. https:// www.racked.com/2018/6/5/17380662/size-numbers-average-woman -plus-market.

5. Denney, J. T., Zhang, Z., Gorman, B. K., and Cooley, C. "Substance Use, Mental Well-Being, and Suicide Ideation by Sexual Orientation among US Adults." *Sexual and Gender Minority Health* (*Advances in*

Medical Sociology) 21 (January 15, 2021): 39–63. https://doi.org/10
.1108/s1057-629020210000021008.

6. Zane, Z. "Who Really Practices Polyamory?" *Rolling Stone*, November 12, 2018. https://www.rollingstone.com/culture/culture-features
/polyamory-bisexual-study-pansexual-754696/.

7. Levine, E. C., Herbenick, D., Martinez, O., Fu, T.-C., and Dodge, B. "Open Relationships, Nonconsensual Nonmonogamy, and Monogamy among U.S. Adults: Findings from the 2012 National Survey of Sexual Health and Behavior." *Archives of Sexual Behavior* 47, no. 5 (2018): 1439–50. https://doi.org/10.1007/s10508-018-1178-7.

8. Oswald, J. "Companies Are Leaving Neurodiversity out of Their DEI Conversations—and That's a Mistake." *Fast Company*, July 27, 2021. https://www.fastcompany.com/90646292/companies-are-leaving
-neurodiversity-out-of-their-dei-conversations-and-thats-a-mistake.

Chapter 6

1. Hicks, M. "The Long History behind the Google Walkout." *The Verge*, November 9, 2018. https://www.theverge.com/2018/11/9/18078664
/google-walkout-history-tech-strikes-labor-organizing.

2. Schiffer, Z. "Everlane Customer Experience Workers Say They Were Illegally Laid Off." *The Verge*, April 2, 2020. https://www.theverge.com
/2020/4/2/21069279/everlane-customer-experience-union-majority
-illegal.

3. Gawlak, E. *Being Black in Corporate America: An Intersectional Exploration* (Chicago: Coqual, 2019).

4. Stropoli, R. "Are We Really More Productive Working from Home?" *Chicago Booth Review*, August 18, 2021. https://www.chicagobooth.edu
/review/are-we-really-more-productive-working-home.

Chapter 8

1. Dover, T., Major, B., and Kaiser, C. "Diversity Policies Rarely Make Companies Fairer, and They Feel Threatening to White Men." *Harvard*

Business Review, January 4, 2016. https://hbr.org/2016/01/diversity
-policies-dont-help-women-or-minorities-and-they-make-white-men
-feel-threatened.

Chapter 9

1. Human capital is the perceived economic value of an employee's skills and experience, regardless of any other characteristic.

Chapter 11

1. Ennis, D. "Don't Let That Rainbow Logo Fool You: These 9 Corporations Donated Millions to Anti-Gay Politicians." *Forbes*, December 10, 2021. https://www.forbes.com/sites/dawnstaceyennis/2019/06/24/dont-let-that-rainbow-logo-fool-you-these-corporations-donated-millions-to-anti-gay-politicians/?sh=650cafc514a6.

2. Most Central American countries gained independence in September and October, which is why these are the dates for Latinx/Hispanic Heritage Month.

3. Harrison, S. "Five Years of Tech Diversity Reports—and Little Progress." *Wired*, October 1, 2019. https://www.wired.com/story/five-years-tech-diversity-reports-little-progress/.

4. Thomas, R. "The Tech Industry Is Failing People with Disabilities and Chronic Illnesses." *Medium*, October 1, 2019. https://medium.com/@racheltho/the-tech-industry-is-failing-people-with-disabilities-and-chronic-illnesses-8e8aa17937f3.

5. Accenture. *Equality = Innovation: Getting to Equal 2019: Creating a Culture That Drives Innovation*, 2019. https://www.accenture.com/_acnmedia/thought-leadership-assets/pdf/accenture-equality-equals-innovation-gender-equality-research-report-iwd-2019.pdf.

6. Flournoy, A. "What Does It Mean to Acknowledge the Past?" *New York Times*, December 31, 2016. https://www.nytimes.com/2016/12/31/opinion/sunday/what-does-it-mean-to-acknowledge-the-past.html.

Resources:
What to Do Next

You've made it to the end of the book! This is not the time to put your pen down, put this book on the shelf, and never look at it again. Incorporate the ideas you've learned here into your own DEI actions or the actions you take at work. Have conversations with your leadership. If you are a leader, enact meaningful change and leverage DEI activities that run deeper than just checking boxes.

◻

DEI is a process that never ends. We're constantly learning new things about the world and the discrimination individuals face, and as we continue to become a more intersectional planet, new opportunities for inclusion arise. A sustained education in global news, human issues, and workplace best practices will equip you for the next iteration of the modern workplace.

◻

The following are some resources to keep you going. Even as I started to pull these lists together, I noticed the significant number of texts and resources created by white individuals or that failed to consider an intersectional perspective. Although these resources are not perfect or comprehensive, I have tried to prioritize intersectional perspectives wherever possible.

BIAS AND KNOWLEDGE GAPS

- ▶ Harvard Implicit Association Test—https://implicit .harvard.edu/
- ▶ Mahzarin Banaji, *Blindspot: Hidden Biases of Good People*

RACIAL DIVERSITY CONVERSATIONS

- ▶ Racial Equity Resource Guide Glossary—http://www .racialequityresourceguide.org/about/glossary
- ▶ Robin DiAngelo, *White Fragility: Why It's So Hard for White People to Talk about Racism*
- ▶ Ibram X. Kendi, *How to Be an Antiracist*
- ▶ Ijeoma Oluo, *So You Want to Talk about Race*
- ▶ Frank H. Wu, *Yellow*
- ▶ Ta-Nehisi Coates, *Between the World and Me*
- ▶ Leo R. Chavez, *The Latino Threat*
- ▶ Tiffany Jana, *Subtle Acts of Exclusion: How to Understand, Identify, and Stop Microaggressions*
- ▶ Minda Harts, *Right Within: How to Heal from Racial Trauma in the Workplace*
- ▶ Andre Henry, *All the White Friends I Couldn't Keep*
- ▶ Roxanne Dunbar-Ortiz, *An Indigenous Peoples' History of the United States*

LGBTQIA+ CONVERSATIONS

- ▶ Matthew Riemer and Leighton Brown, *We Are Everywhere: Protest, Power, and Pride in the History of Queer Liberation*
- ▶ Laurie Marhoefer, *Racism and the Making of Gay Rights*

- Rasheed Newson, *My Government Means to Kill Me* (fiction, yet phenomenal)
- Ellen Pao, *Reset: My Fight for Inclusion and Lasting Change*

POWER AND PRIVILEGE

- Isabel Wilkerson, *Caste: The Origins of Our Discontents*
- Diversity Toolkit (for leading conversations)—https://msw.usc.edu/mswusc-blog/diversity-workshop-guide-to-discussing-identity-power-and-privilege/
- Paulo Freire, *Pedagogy of the Oppressed*
- Allan G. Johnson, *Privilege, Power, and Difference*

DISABILITY

- Joseph P. Shapiro, *No Pity: People with Disabilities Forging a New Civil Rights Movement*
- Devon Price, *Unmasking Autism*
- Simo Vehmas and Nick Watson, *Moral Wrongs, Disadvantages, and Disability: A Critique of Critical Disability Studies*
- D. Dunn and E. Andrews, "Person-First and Identity-First Language," *American Psychologist* 70, no. 3, 255–64
- Haben Girma, "I Am Harvard Law's First Deafblind Graduate. Here's What College Is Like for Students with Disabilities," *CNBC make it.*
- Judith Heumann with Kristen Joiner, *Being Heumann: An Unrepentant Memoir of a Disability Rights Activist*
- Alice Wong, *Disability Visibility: First-Person Stories from the Twenty-First Century*
- Jay Timothy Dolmage, *Academic Ableism*
- Eric Garcia, *We're Not Broken: Changing the Autism Conversation*

INCLUSION AND CHANGE

- ▶ Ruchika Tulshyan, *Inclusion on Purpose*
- ▶ Natale Franke, *Built to Belong*
- ▶ DeRay Mckesson, *On the Other Side of Freedom: The Case for Hope*
- ▶ Tiffany Jana and Matthew Freeman, *Overcoming Bias: Building Authentic Relationships across Differences*
- ▶ Tiffany Jana and Ashley Diaz Mejias, with foreword by Jay Coen Gilbert, *Erasing Institutional Bias: How to Create Systemic Change for Organizational Inclusion*

Acknowledgments

This isn't the first book I've written (and I hope it won't be the last), but it was certainly the highest-stakes project. Diversity, equity, and inclusion are deeply personal topics to so many people, and I so desperately wanted to do these topics (and those they impact) true justice. Although I'm not sure I did, as I learn something new about DEI every day and it's been months since I finished the first draft of this manuscript, here's hoping you still learned something new.

■

This book wouldn't have been possible without countless individuals, more than I could ever name here, and I'm grateful to each and every one of them for their contributions to my voice, my confidence, my trailblazing spirit, and my never-ending willingness to be the Challenger. I know that there are dozens of people I've missed in this acknowledgments section; know that I see and honor your work in my life and our community. Never for a second think that I underestimate your contributions.

■

I first need to thank my wife, Kaity. You entered my life before the first words of the book proposal that led to the text you hold today had even hit paper. Every single step of the way, you have been its number-one champion, even as I stressed about (and procrastinated on) the final content that made the manuscript. Your devotion and commitment to our relationship motivates me to be my very best every day.

※

To my literary agent, Rachel Beck of Liza Dawson Associates, who believed in my writing even when my first book idea didn't sell. This book exists only because of how hard you fought for me. Every single rejection email only fueled our fire to find the people who cared about this book as much as we did. Your efforts paid off! Here we are!

※

To the team at Berrett-Koehler, especially my editor Sarah, thank you for everything. My biggest fear entering the publishing process was that this book would lose its teeth before it hit shelves. You understood why this book's teeth was what made it impactful, and you fought with me to make sure that the message stayed strong.

※

To Rea Frey of Writeway, a fellow author, for the power of my book proposal and for the email that started this whole process. Your insights and dedication helped provide the format that would make publishers fall in love with this book.

※

To the small but mighty team behind my entrepreneurial pursuits, thank you for always being there. Thank you for supporting a girl with big dreams who always takes on too much and asks the world of you. You've made these big dreams possible.

※

To my team at Google, I had no idea that my pivot to staffing would lead not only to the career I've long been waiting for but also to the team that I'd call family.

To those at work who have had my back and been my shield and armor in battles for diversity, equity, and inclusion—this journey would not have been possible nor gone half as far without you. As we cried together, traded angry pings and texts, or started our very own version of a revolution, your energy and effort changed the lives of people around us every single day. Alexandria, Juliana, Haley M and Haley H, Kris and KC, Melissa, Jenna, Jen and Eric, Betina and Johnie, the entire SDS DEI community and Pande DEI Circle team—you're the fire that keeps this story burning.

To the DEI leaders in various communities in my life, thank you for your tireless work to making this world even marginally better than it is now. To Kait Masters, who fights for the marginalized every day, regardless of your own energy level. To Natalie Franke for giving my passion for DEI its first global stage. To Tiffany Tolliver for every voice memo we've traded and every "Did they really post that?" text we've shared. To Noel Dolan for every moment you have spent fighting for others even through your own trials. To Reina Pomeroy for teaching me to prioritize happiness and never compromise my own joy. To Mo Speer for your willingness to learn and the way you turned around and pulled others up with you.

To my mentors for every moment of inspiration and every reminder to rest in between the fighting. To Dr. Kevin Danley for taking on a student juggling a book manuscript along with doctoral writing, and being my biggest academic cheerleader and first doctoral friend. To Dr. Vicki Baker for being the first to see this fight in me and encouraging me to stay true to myself always. To Dr. John Carlson for being my undergraduate thesis advisor and helping me produce my first written DEI work. To Dr. Carrie Booth Walling for the inspiration for my first published paper and the reminder that fighting for the underdog is *always* the right choice. To Kris Ingle, Johnny Mauro, and KC Coplan for being the kind of leaders I aspire to be and for prioritizing the relationship over the business every single time. To Kellie Fitzgerald for every honest conversation and every moment of real unvarnished and truthful career advice. To Heather Cain for a mentor relationship turned personal as we both went through the same massive life change.

▦

To all the managers who have ever fought with me or fired me, in large part you made the passion for this book burn even brighter.

▦

To my friends, you know who you are. You've read every text, seen every screenshot, choked back laughter and your own rage as my eyes rolled harder and harder. You've listened to my endless monologues for why x scenario was bullshit or why y thing on the internet never should have existed in the first place. You're the lifeblood that keeps this battle raging on inside me, no matter how difficult.

▦

To Mary Marantz, the girl in the trailer. Your story shattered my soul and taught me the power of raw honesty. It *always* started with dirt.

▦

To my family, both blood and chosen. To Granny and Grampy, to Vickie and Evandro and Chris, to Jan, to Ginny and Cyndi, to Kayleigh and Lindsey and David, to Sarah and Taylor. Your strength in every moment of my life, no matter what it threw at us, made us stand deeper in love and taught us to prioritize what matters most.

▦

And last but not least, to Briggs. When I fell in love with Kaity, you were part of the package deal, little guy. I had no idea that you'd become my favorite coworker, my most helpful researcher, and the best four-legged friend I could ever have asked for.

Index

Love This Book?

Don't forget to leave a review! Every review matters.
You can also

- ▶ Request a copy of this book at your local library.
- ▶ Send a copy to a friend with your notes inside.
- ▶ Encourage your workplace book club or your team to read and discuss this book.
- ▶ Organize a panel to discuss and debate this book's contents.

I thank you endlessly.

About the Author

Dannie Lynn Fountain (Murphy) is a passionate storyteller dedicated to helping companies focus on people. By day, she's a staffer at Google hiring the world's most talented software engineers; by night, she supports clients and brands with HR-focused diversity, equity, and inclusion strategies. She's also a multipassionate human—beyond  working in HR, Dannie Lynn is an academic, a licensed Enrolled Agent, and the founder of the #sidehustlegal movement.

Dannie Lynn resides in Seattle with her attorney wife and their dog, Briggs. When not working, she's reading books and scrolling booktok, traveling the world, swimming and rowing, or stirring up trouble.

You can connect further with Dannie Lynn on Instagram @dannielynnfountain or on her website, www.danniefountain.com.

◈ Berrett–Koehler
BK̄ Publishers

Berrett-Koehler is an independent publisher dedicated to an ambitious mission: *Connecting people and ideas to create a world that works for all.*

Our publications span many formats, including print, digital, audio, and video. We also offer online resources, training, and gatherings. And we will continue expanding our products and services to advance our mission.

We believe that the solutions to the world's problems will come from all of us, working at all levels: in our society, in our organizations, and in our own lives. Our publications and resources offer pathways to creating a more just, equitable, and sustainable society. They help people make their organizations more humane, democratic, diverse, and effective (and we don't think there's any contradiction there). And they guide people in creating positive change in their own lives and aligning their personal practices with their aspirations for a better world.

And we strive to practice what we preach through what we call "The BK Way." At the core of this approach is *stewardship,* a deep sense of responsibility to administer the company for the benefit of all of our stakeholder groups, including authors, customers, employees, investors, service providers, sales partners, and the communities and environment around us. Everything we do is built around stewardship and our other core values of *quality, partnership, inclusion,* and *sustainability.*

This is why Berrett-Koehler is the first book publishing company to be both a B Corporation (a rigorous certification) and a benefit corporation (a for-profit legal status), which together require us to adhere to the highest standards for corporate, social, and environmental performance. And it is why we have instituted many pioneering practices (which you can learn about at www.bkconnection.com), including the Berrett-Koehler Constitution, the Bill of Rights and Responsibilities for BK Authors, and our unique Author Days.

We are grateful to our readers, authors, and other friends who are supporting our mission. We ask you to share with us examples of how BK publications and resources are making a difference in your lives, organizations, and communities at www.bkconnection.com/impact.

Dear reader,

Thank you for picking up this book and welcome to the worldwide BK community! You're joining a special group of people who have come together to create positive change in their lives, organizations, and communities.

What's BK all about?

Our mission is to connect people and ideas to create a world that works for all.

Why? Our communities, organizations, and lives get bogged down by old paradigms of self-interest, exclusion, hierarchy, and privilege. But we believe that can change. That's why we seek the leading experts on these challenges—and share their actionable ideas with you.

A welcome gift

To help you get started, we'd like to offer you a **free copy** of one of our bestselling ebooks:

www.bkconnection.com/welcome

When you claim your **free ebook**, you'll also be subscribed to our blog.

Our freshest insights

Access the best new tools and ideas for leaders at all levels on our blog at ideas.bkconnection.com.

Sincerely,

Your friends at Berrett-Koehler